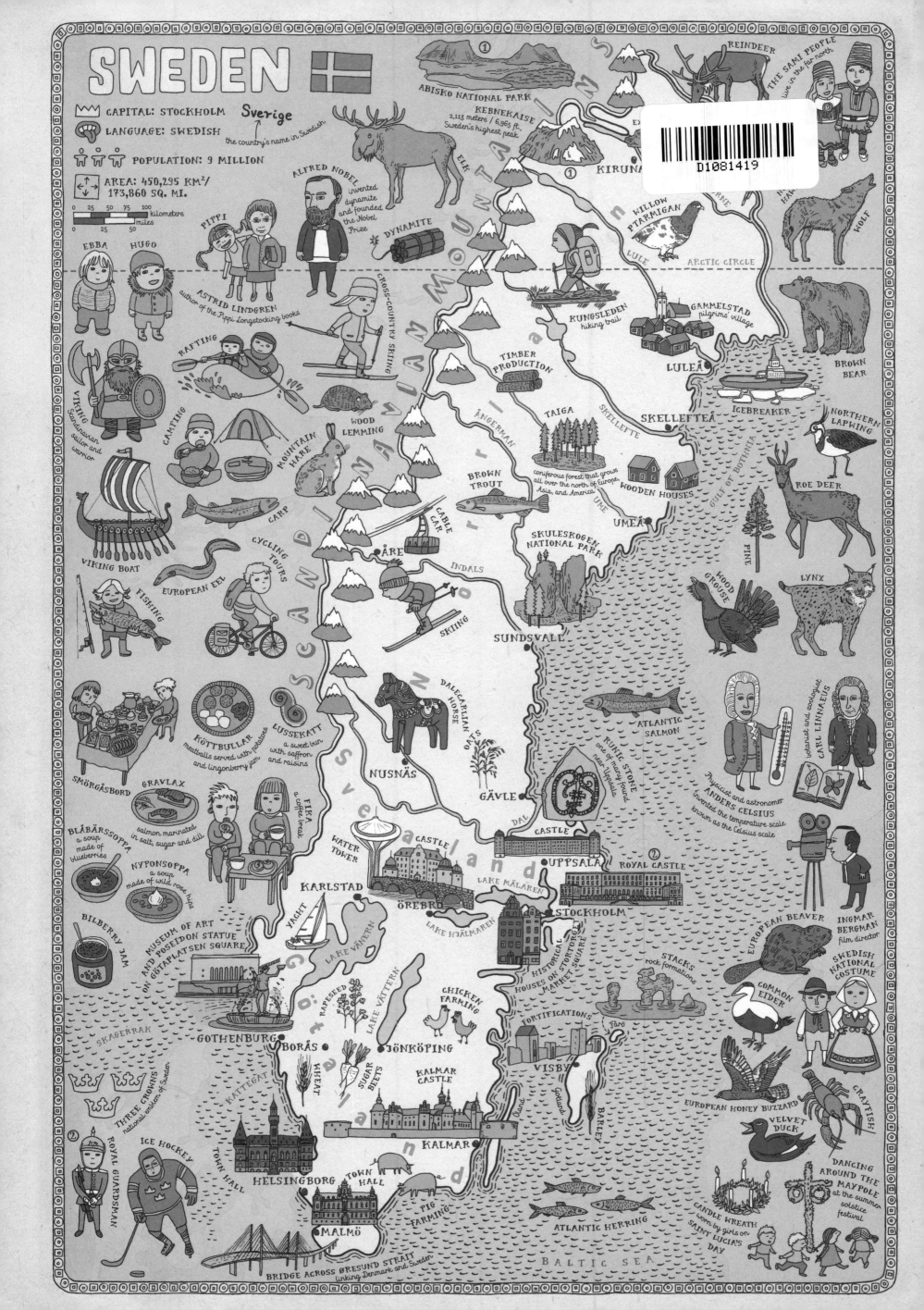

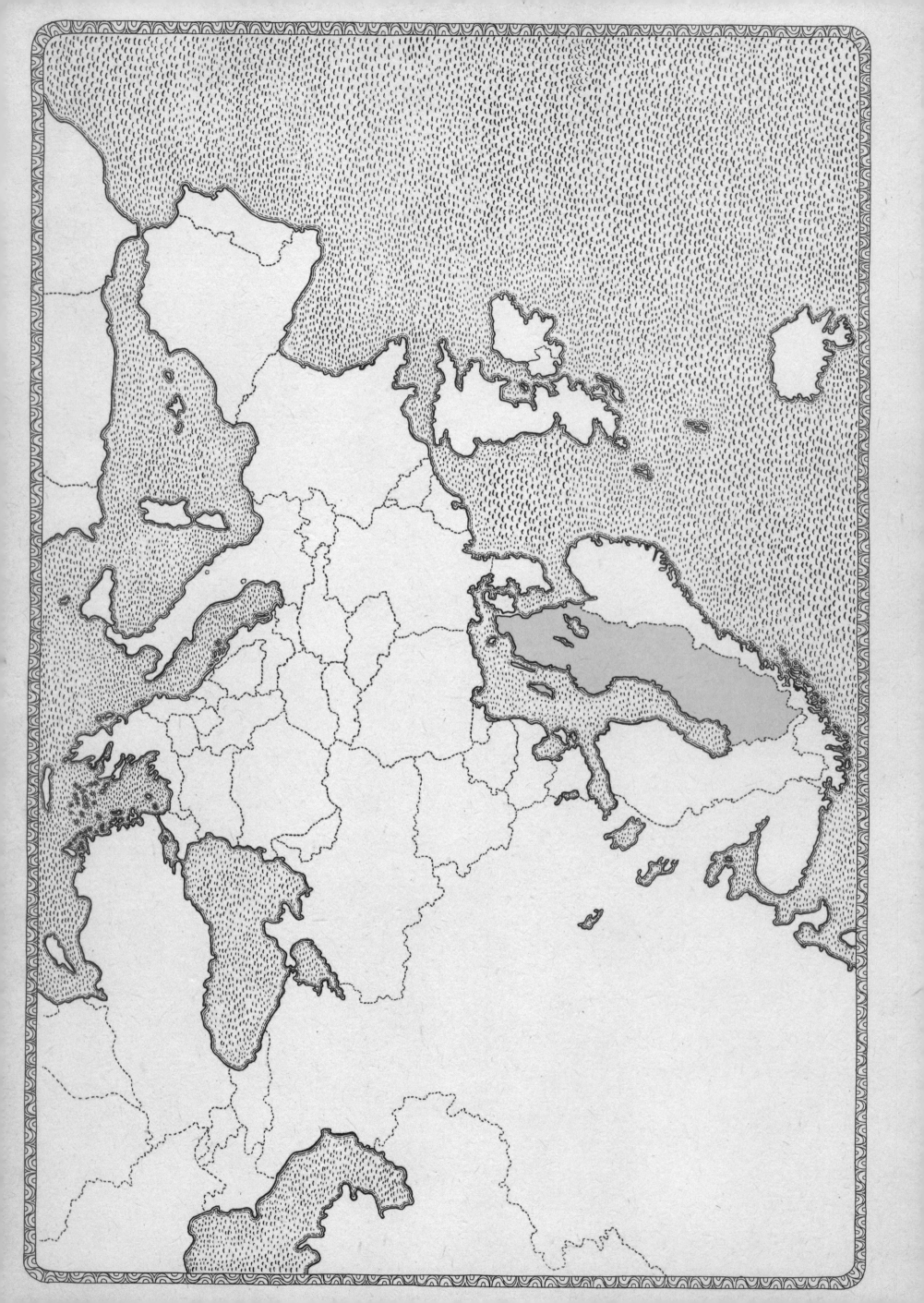

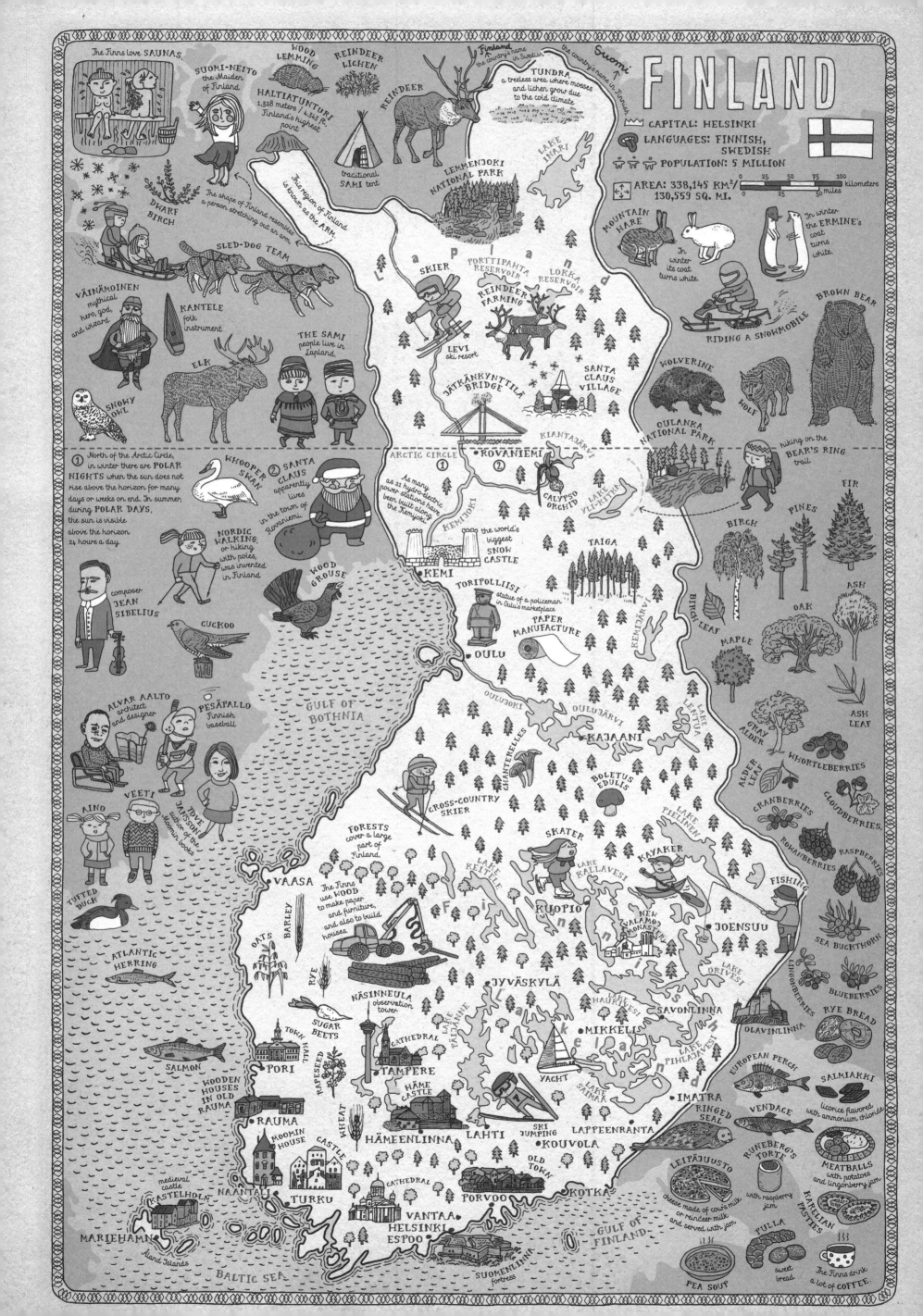

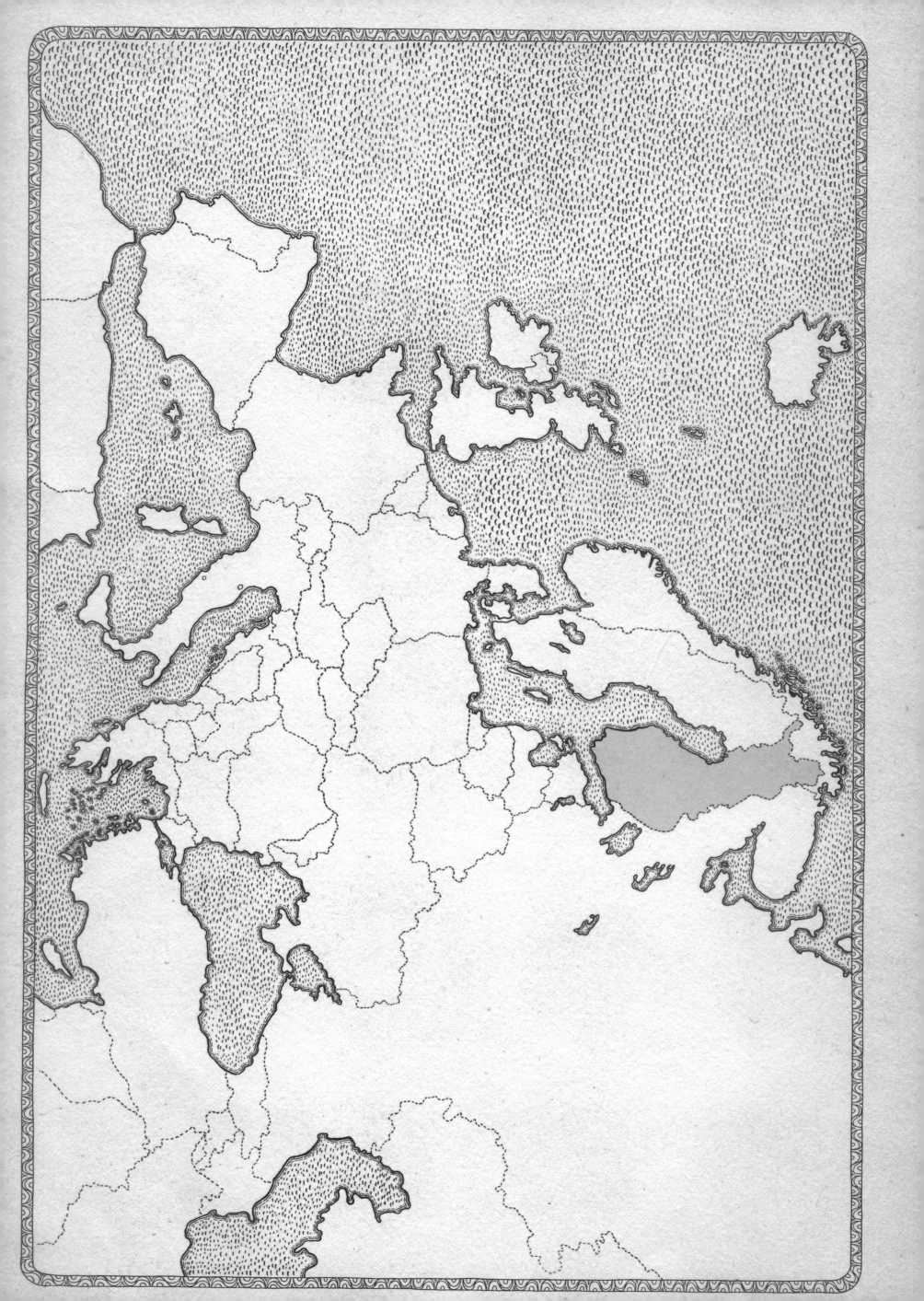

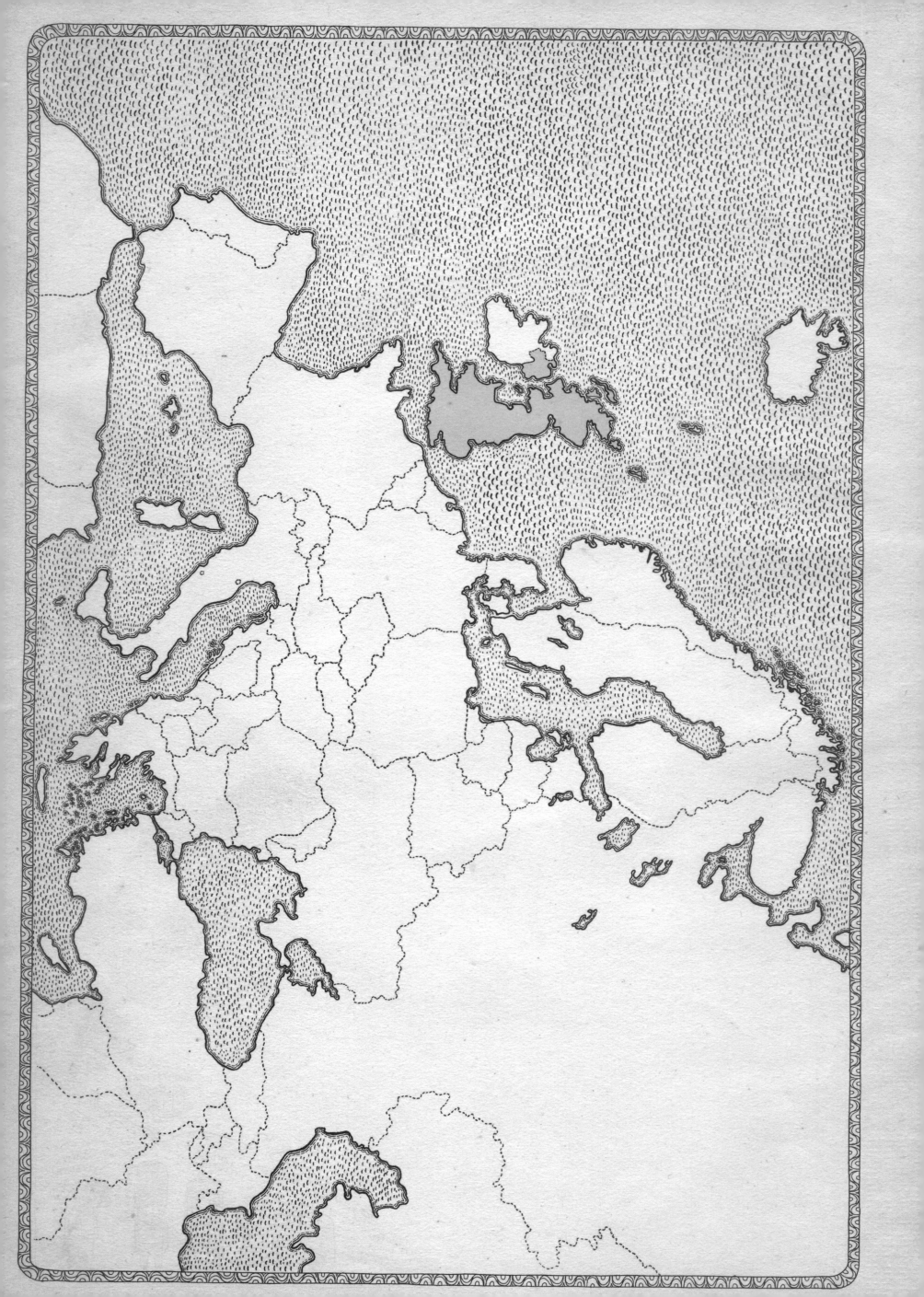

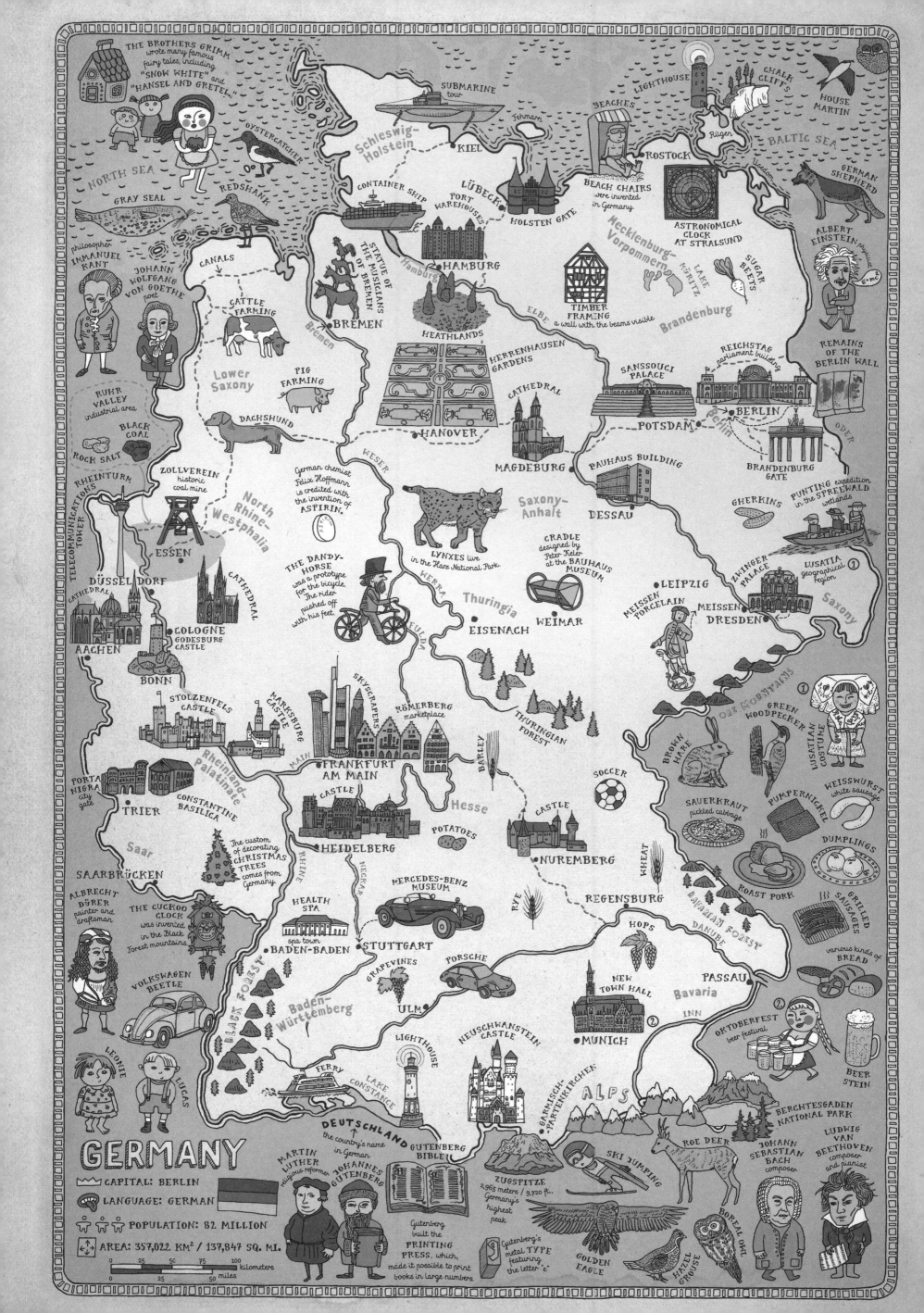

THE BROTHERS GRIMM wrote many famous fairy tales, including "SNOW WHITE" and "HANSEL AND GRETEL."

NORTH SEA

GRAY SEAL

OYSTERCATCHER

REDSHANK

philosopher IMMANUEL KANT

JOHANN WOLFGANG VON GOETHE poet

CANALS

CATTLE FARMING

Schleswig-Holstein

KIEL

SUBMARINE tour

Fehmarn

LIGHTHOUSE

BEACHES

BEACH CHAIRS were invented in Germany.

CHALK CLIFFS

Rügen

HOUSE MARTIN

BALTIC SEA

GERMAN SHEPHERD

ALBERT EINSTEIN physicist
$E=mc^2$

CONTAINER SHIP

LÜBECK

PORT WAREHOUSES

HOLSTEN GATE

ROSTOCK

Mecklenburg-Vorpommern

ASTRONOMICAL CLOCK AT STRALSUND

Usedom

LAKE MÜRITZ

SUGAR BEETS

Hamburg

HAMBURG

STATUE OF THE MUSICIANS OF BREMEN

Bremen

BREMEN

HEATHLANDS

HERRENHAUSEN GARDENS

TIMBER FRAMING a wall with the beams visible

Brandenburg

Elbe

RUHR VALLEY industrial area

BLACK COAL

ROCK SALT

Lower Saxony

PIG FARMING

DACHSHUND

ZOLLVEREIN historic coal mine

RHEINTURM

TELECOMMUNICATIONS TOWER

North Rhine-Westphalia

German chemist Felix Hoffmann is credited with the invention of ASPIRIN.

ASPIRIN

WESER

CATHEDRAL

HANOVER

MAGDEBURG

Saxony-Anhalt

LYNXES live in the Harz National Park.

REICHSTAG parliament building

SANSSOUCI PALACE

BERLIN

Berlin

POTSDAM

BRANDENBURG GATE

REMAINS OF THE BERLIN WALL

ODER

BAUHAUS BUILDING

DESSAU

GHERKINS

PUNTING expedition in the SPREEWALD wetlands

ESSEN

DÜSSELDORF

CATHEDRAL

THE DANDY-HORSE was a prototype for the bicycle. The rider pushed off with his feet.

WERRA

WwW

CRADLE designed by Peter Keler at the BAUHAUS MUSEUM

MEISSEN PORCELAIN

MEISSEN

LEIPZIG

ZWINGER PALACE

LUSATIA geographical region ①

Saxony

AACHEN

CATHEDRAL

COLOGNE

Godesburg Castle

BONN

STOLZENFELS CASTLE

MARKSBURG CASTLE

SKYSCRAPERS

RÖMERBERG marketplace

FULDA

Thuringia

EISENACH

WEIMAR

THURINGIAN FOREST

BARLEY

DRESDEN

ORE MOUNTAINS ①

BROWN HARE

GREEN WOODPECKER

LUSATIAN COSTUME

PORTA NIGRA city gate

CONSTANTINE BASILICA

TRIER

Rheinland-Pfalz

MAIN

FRANKFURT AM MAIN

Hesse

CASTLE

POTATOES

CASTLE

NUREMBERG

SOCCER

SAUERKRAUT pickled cabbage

PUMPERNICKEL

WEISSWURST white sausage

DUMPLINGS

Saar

SAARBRÜCKEN

ALBRECHT DÜRER painter and draftsman

The custom of decorating CHRISTMAS TREES comes from Germany.

HEIDELBERG

RHINE

NECKAR

MERCEDES-BENZ MUSEUM

HEALTH SPA

RYE

CASTLE

REGENSBURG

WHEAT

ROAST PORK

Bavarian Forest

GRILLED SAUSAGES

various kinds of BREAD

THE CUCKOO CLOCK was invented in the Black Forest mountains.

VOLKSWAGEN BEETLE

spa town BADEN-BADEN

STUTTGART

GRAPEVINES

PORSCHE

ULM

Baden-Württemberg

BLACK FOREST

HOPS

DANUBE

NEW TOWN HALL

Bavaria

PASSAU

INN

OKTOBERFEST beer festival ②

BEER STEIN

LEONIE

LUCAS

FERRY

LIGHTHOUSE

LAKE CONSTANCE

NEUSCHWANSTEIN CASTLE

GARMISCH-PARTENKIRCHEN

MUNICH ②

ALPS

ROE DEER

BERCHTESGADEN NATIONAL PARK

BOREAL OWL

LUDWIG VAN BEETHOVEN composer and pianist

GERMANY

⚜ CAPITAL: BERLIN

🗣 LANGUAGE: GERMAN

👪 POPULATION: 82 MILLION

↕ AREA: 357,022 KM² / 137,847 SQ. MI.

0 25 50 75 100 kilometers
0 25 50 miles

MARTIN LUTHER religious reformer

JOHANNES GUTENBERG

DEUTSCHLAND the country's name in German

GUTENBERG BIBLE

Gutenberg built the PRINTING PRESS, which, made it possible to print books in large numbers.

Gutenberg's metal TYPE featuring the letter "e"

ZUGSPITZE 2,963 meters / 9,720 ft., Germany's highest peak

SKI JUMPING

GOLDEN EAGLE

HAZEL GROUSE

JOHANN SEBASTIAN BACH composer

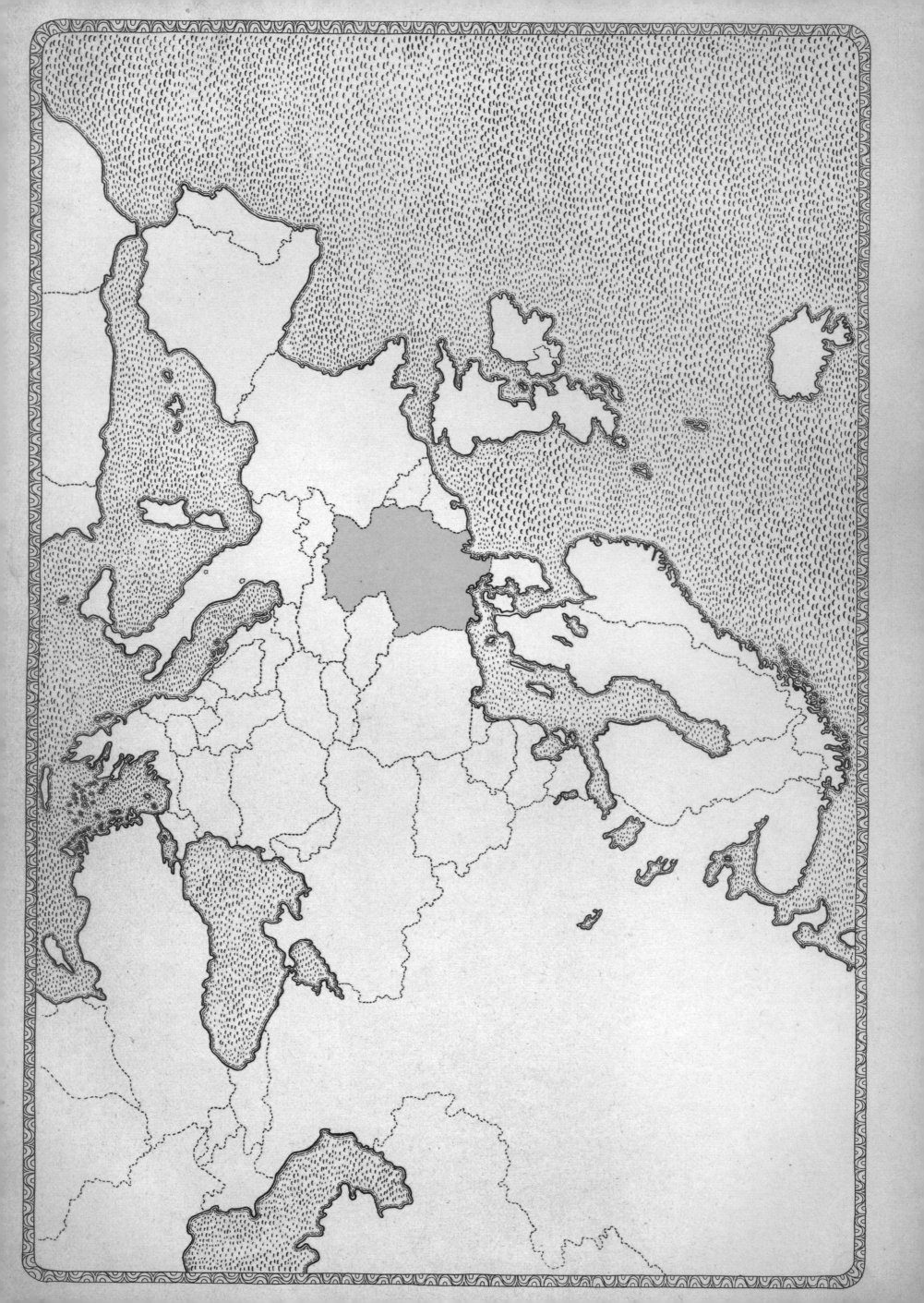

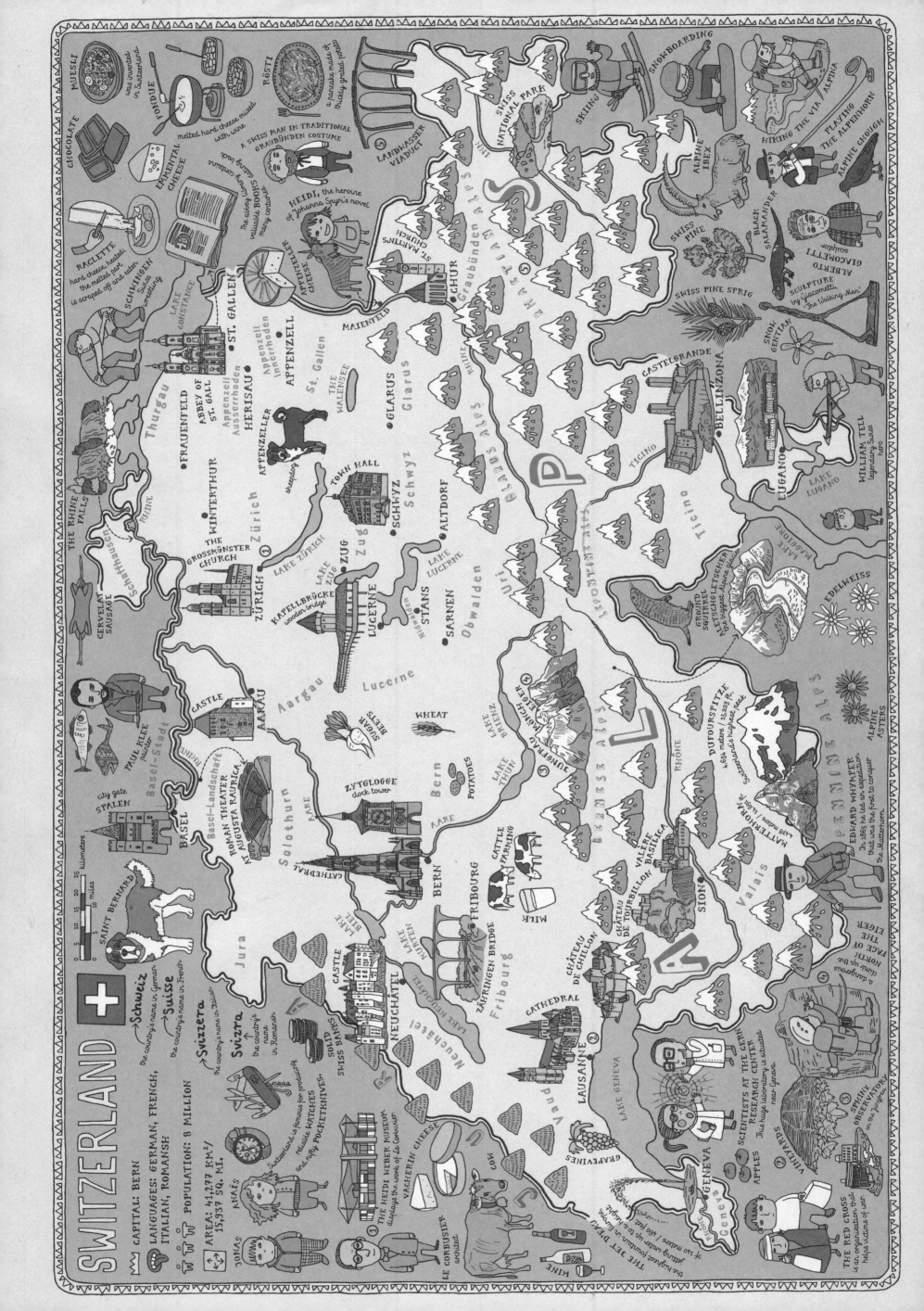

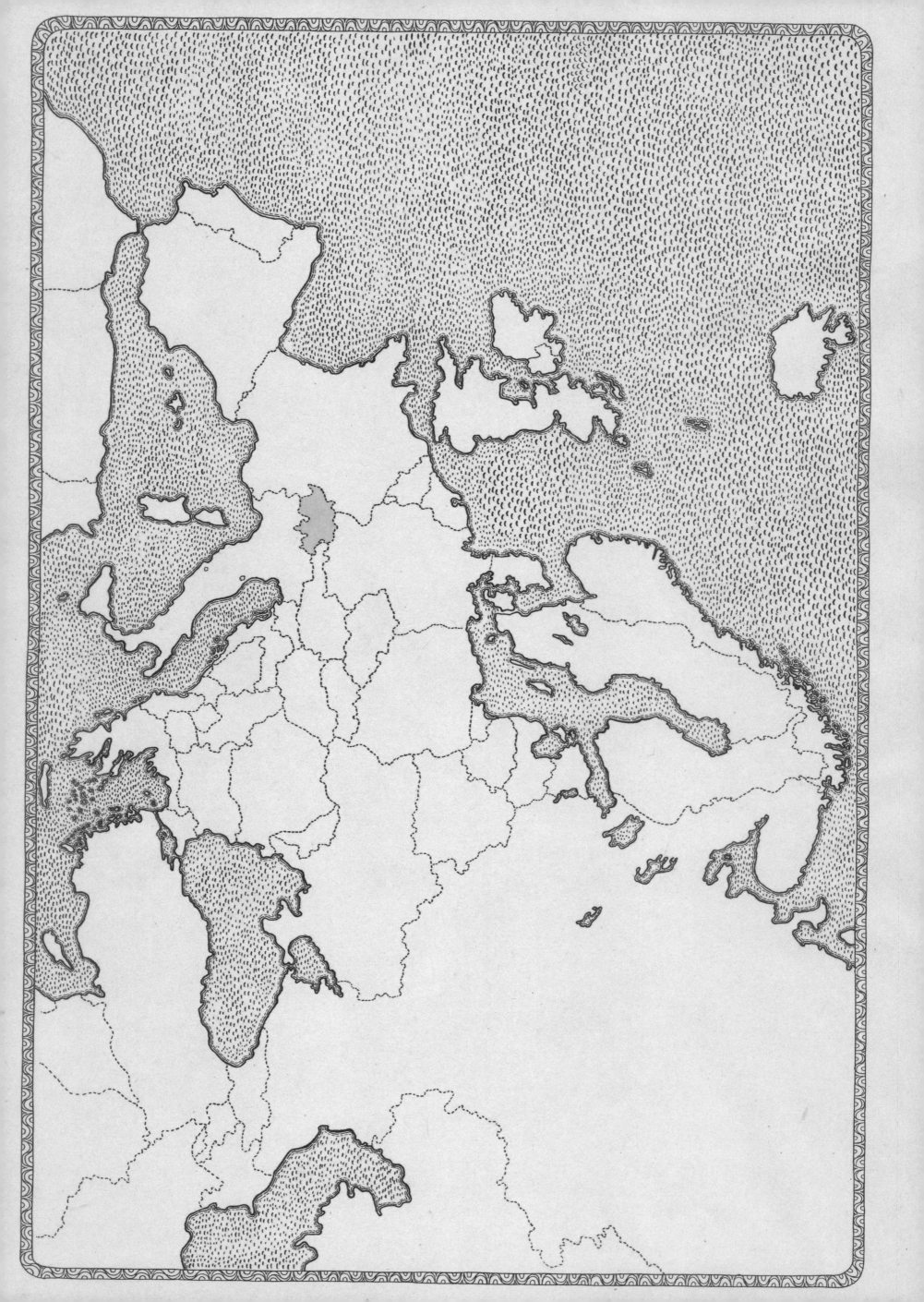

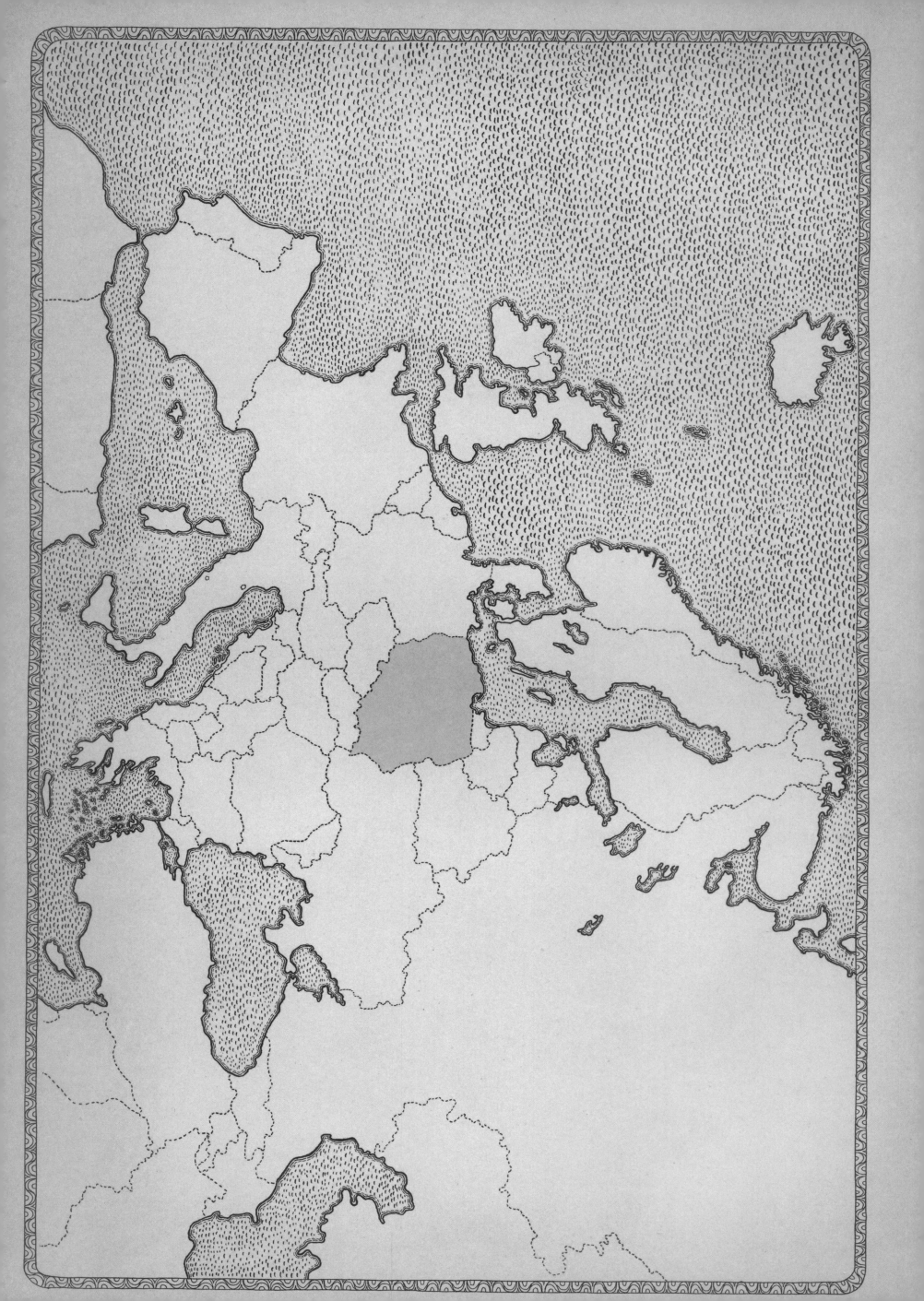

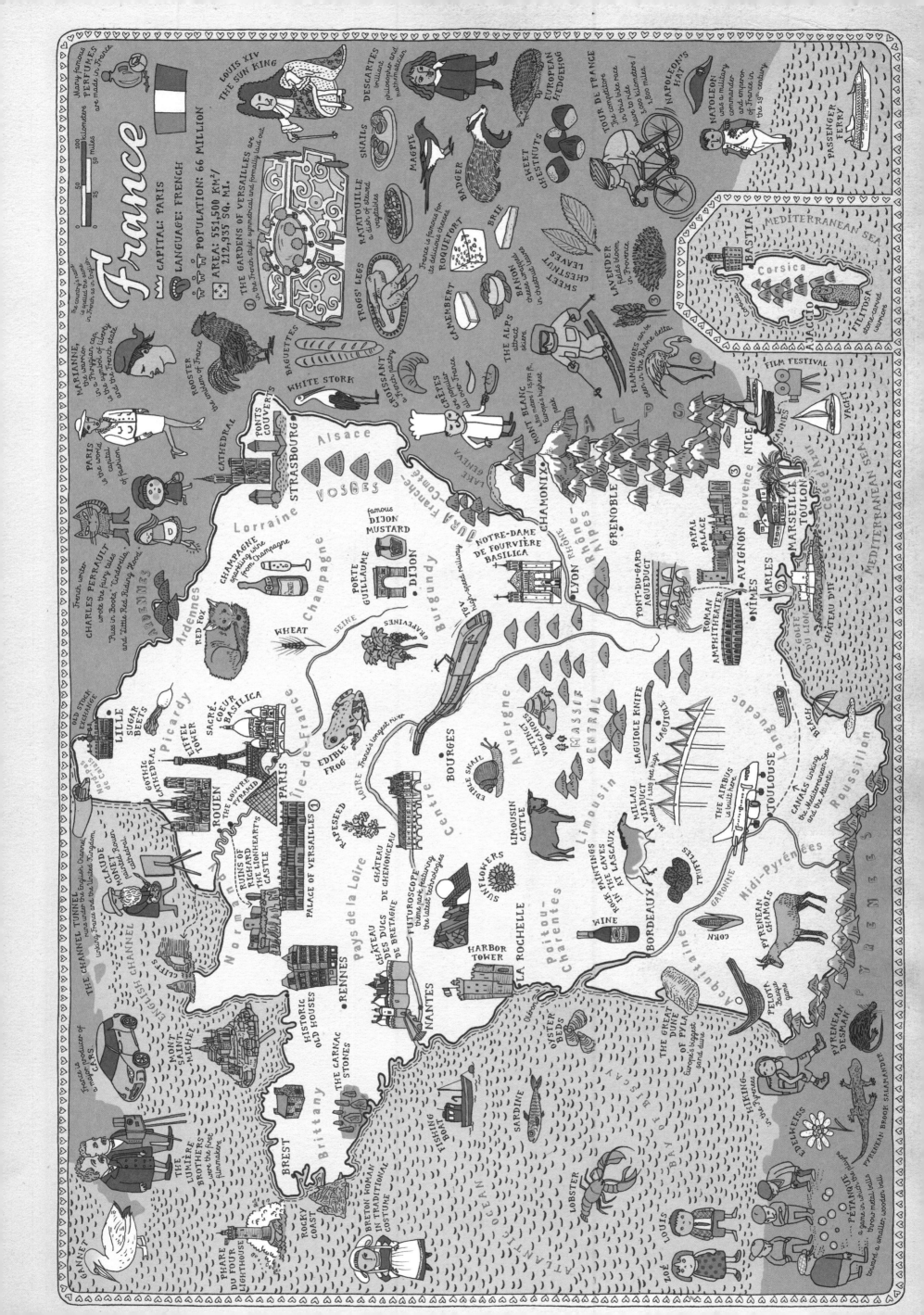

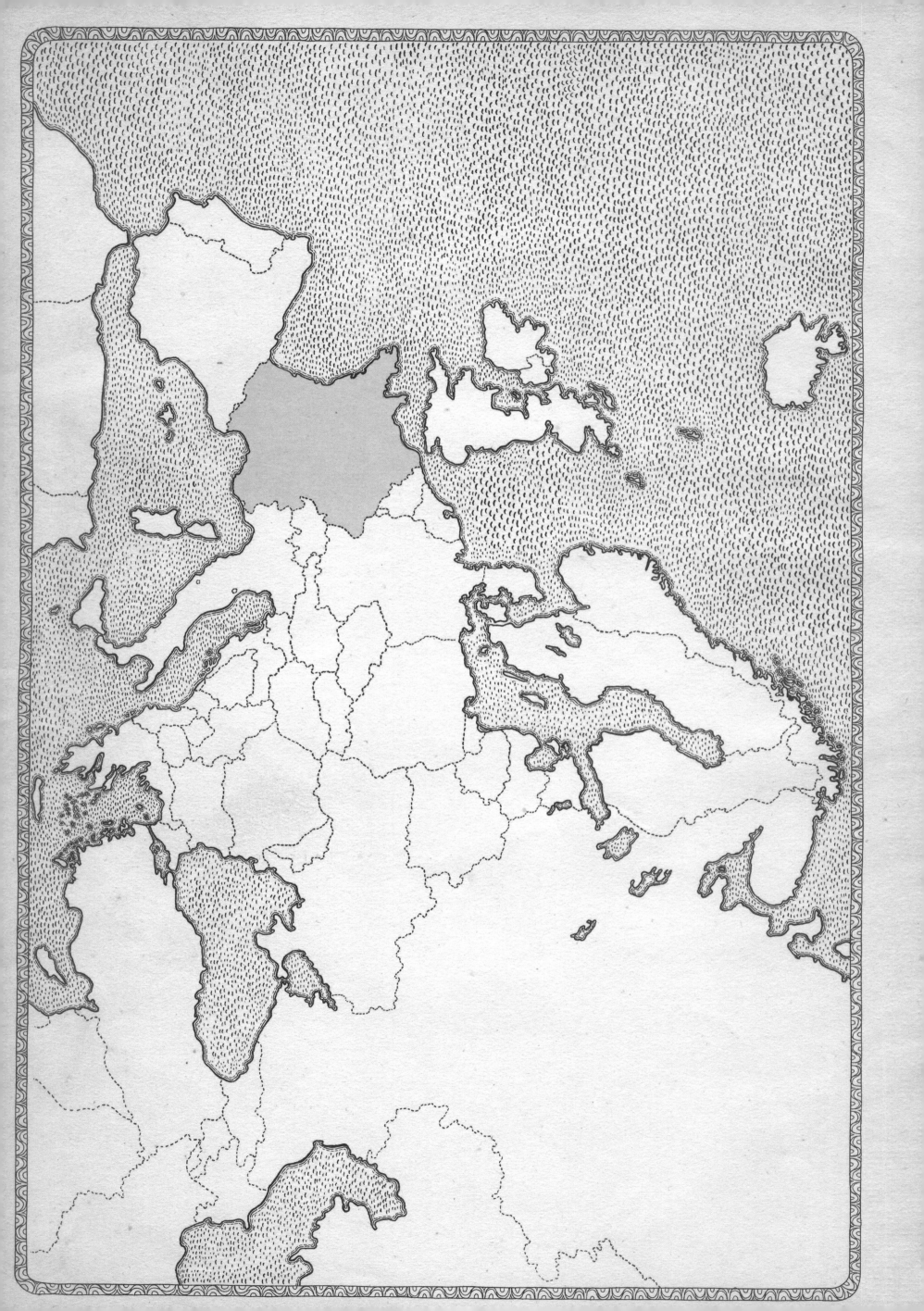

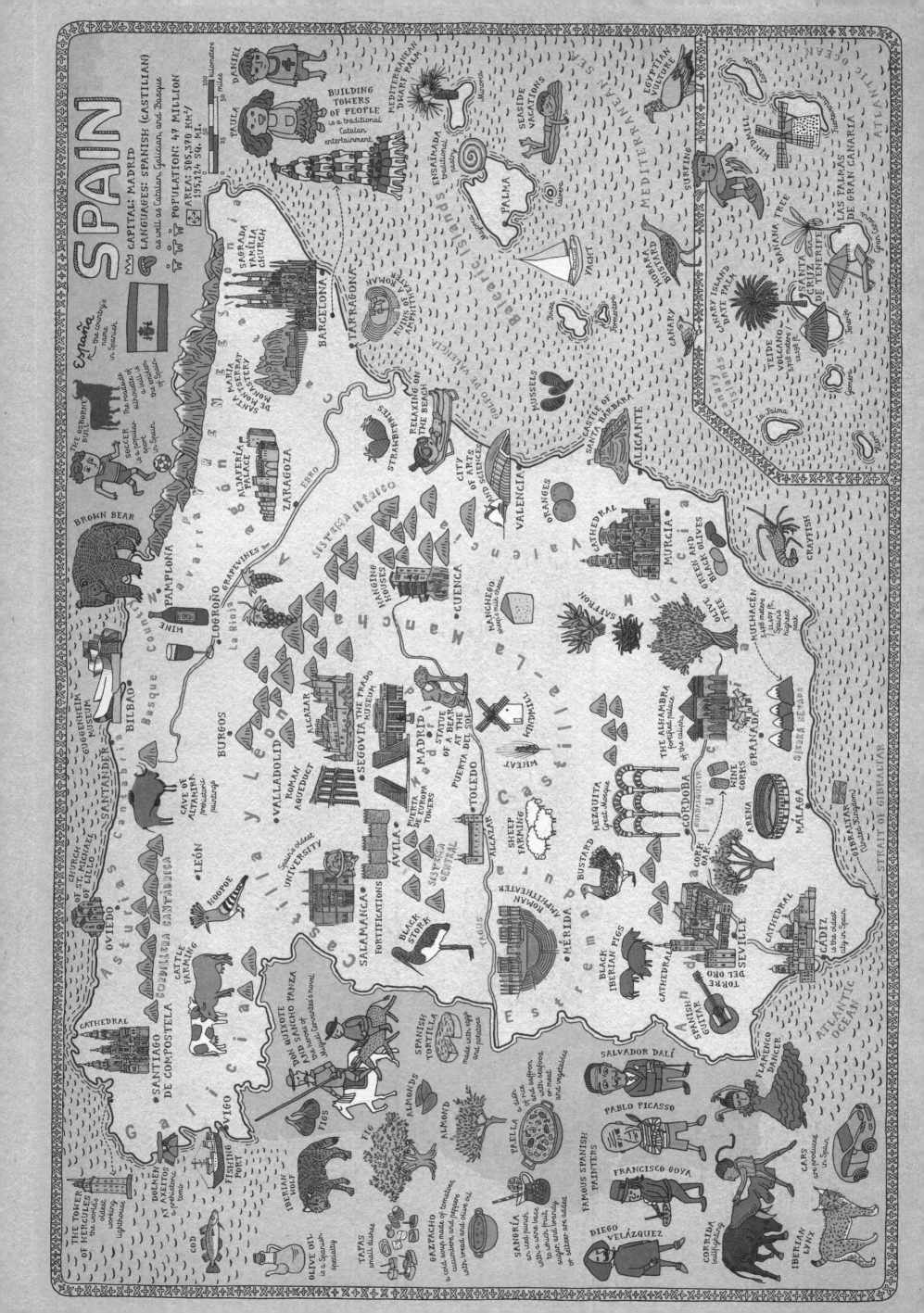

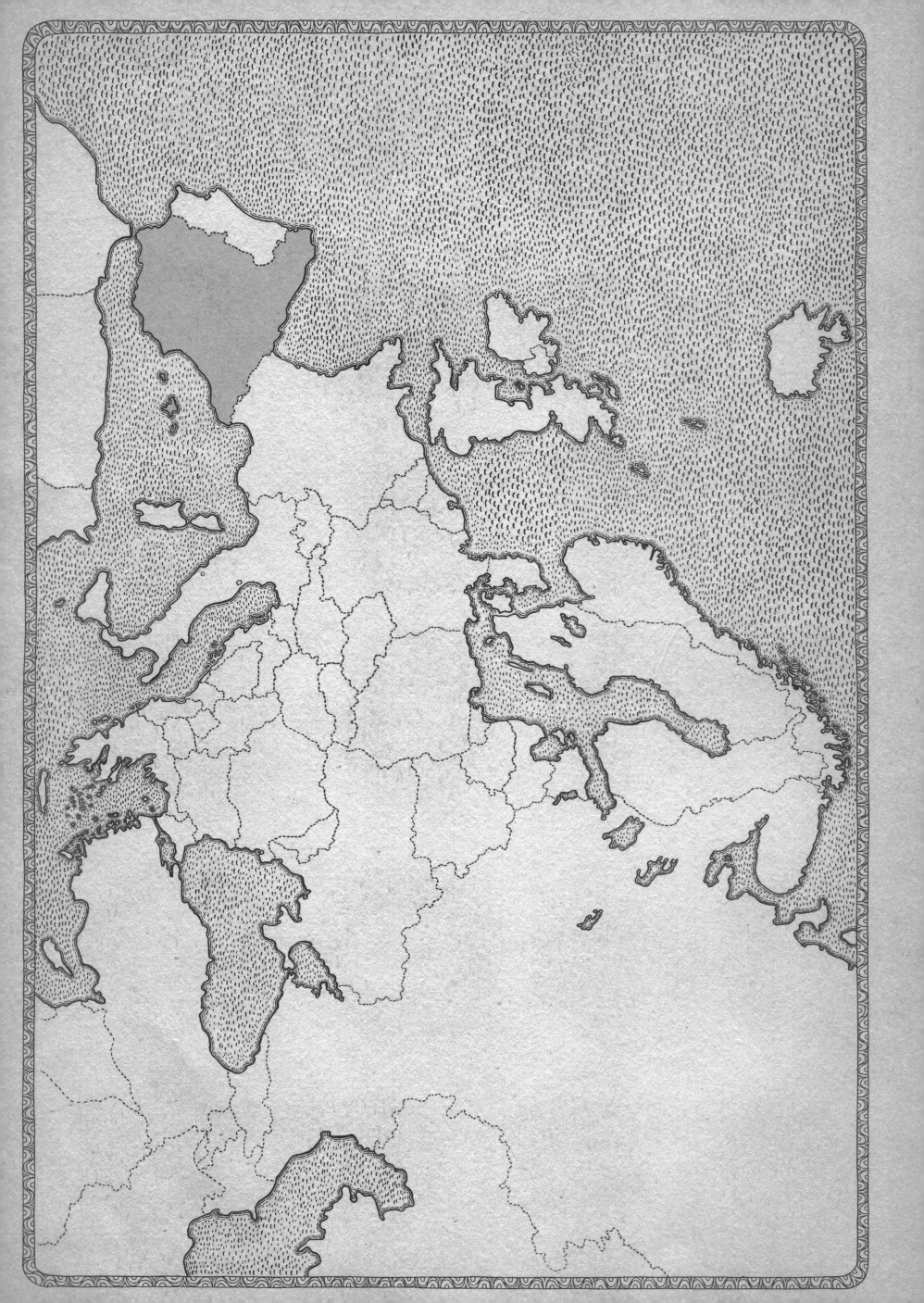

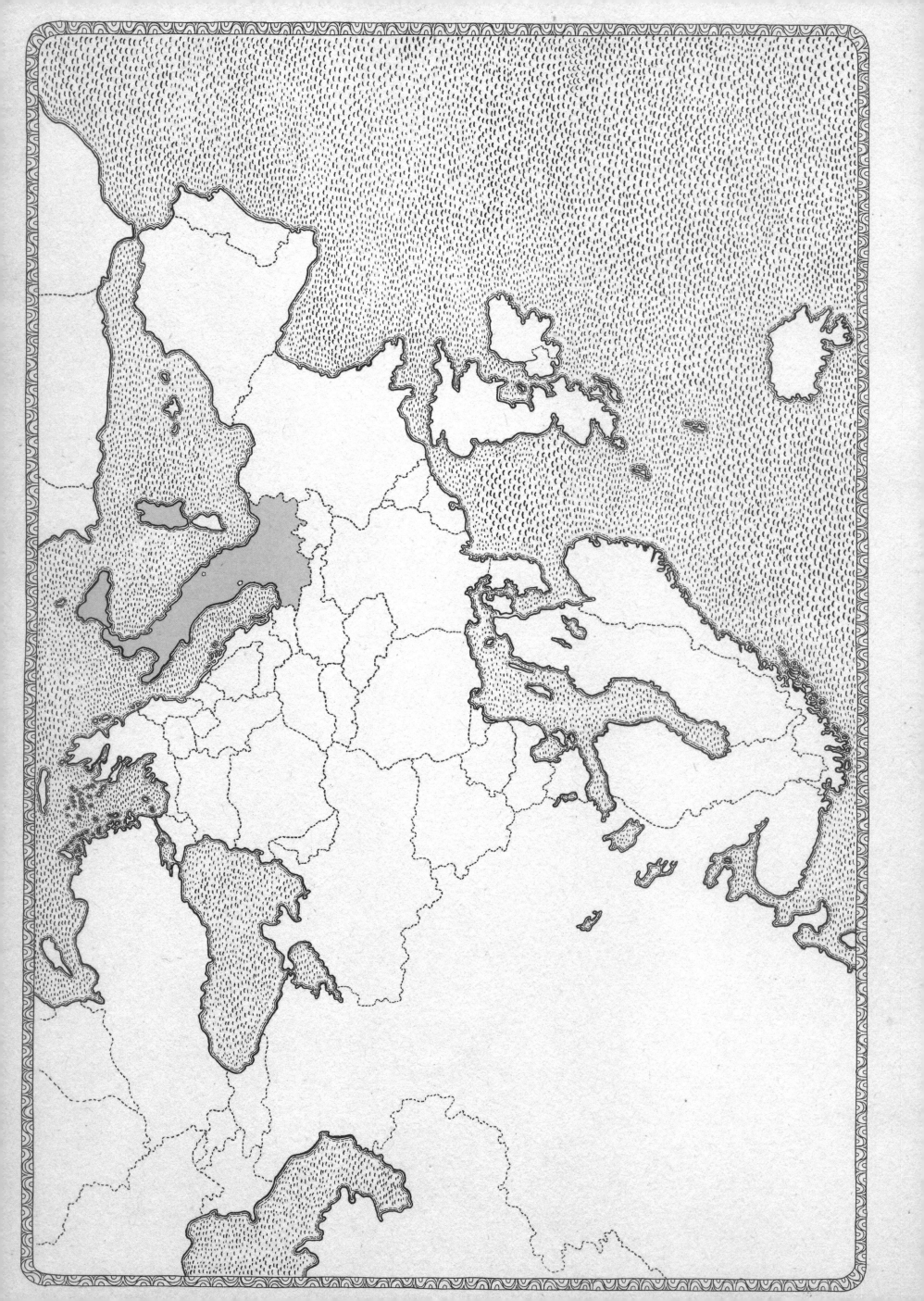

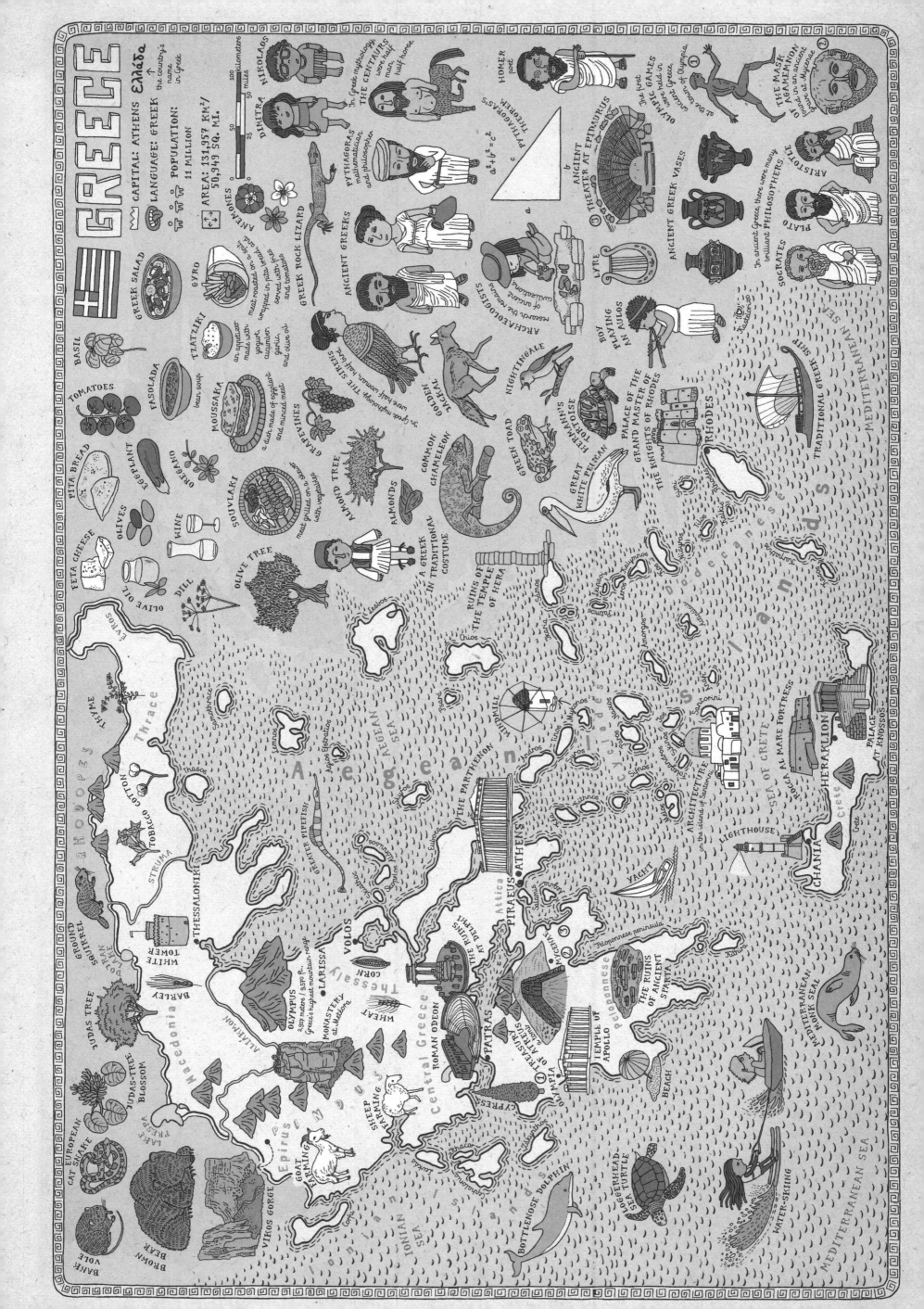

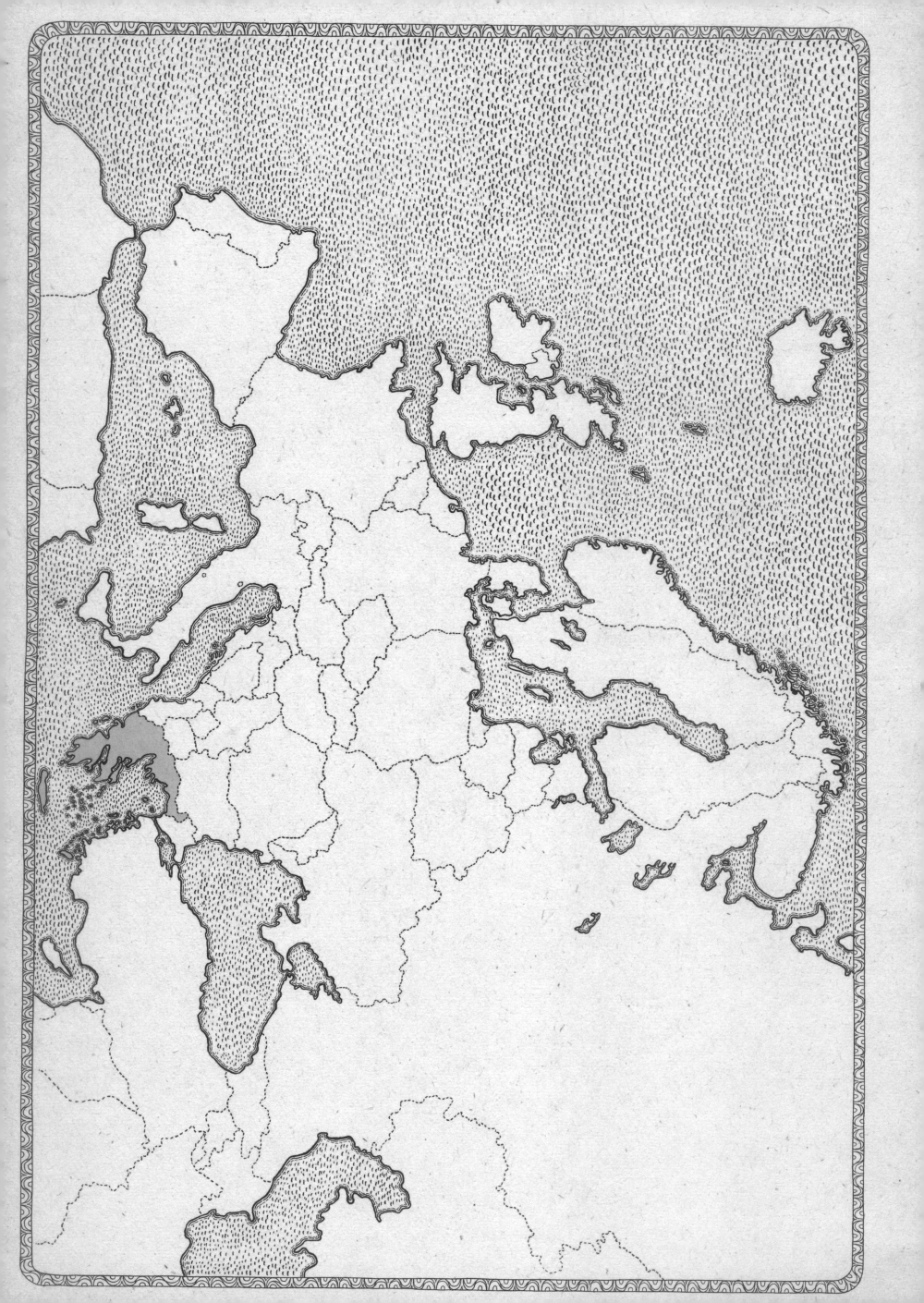

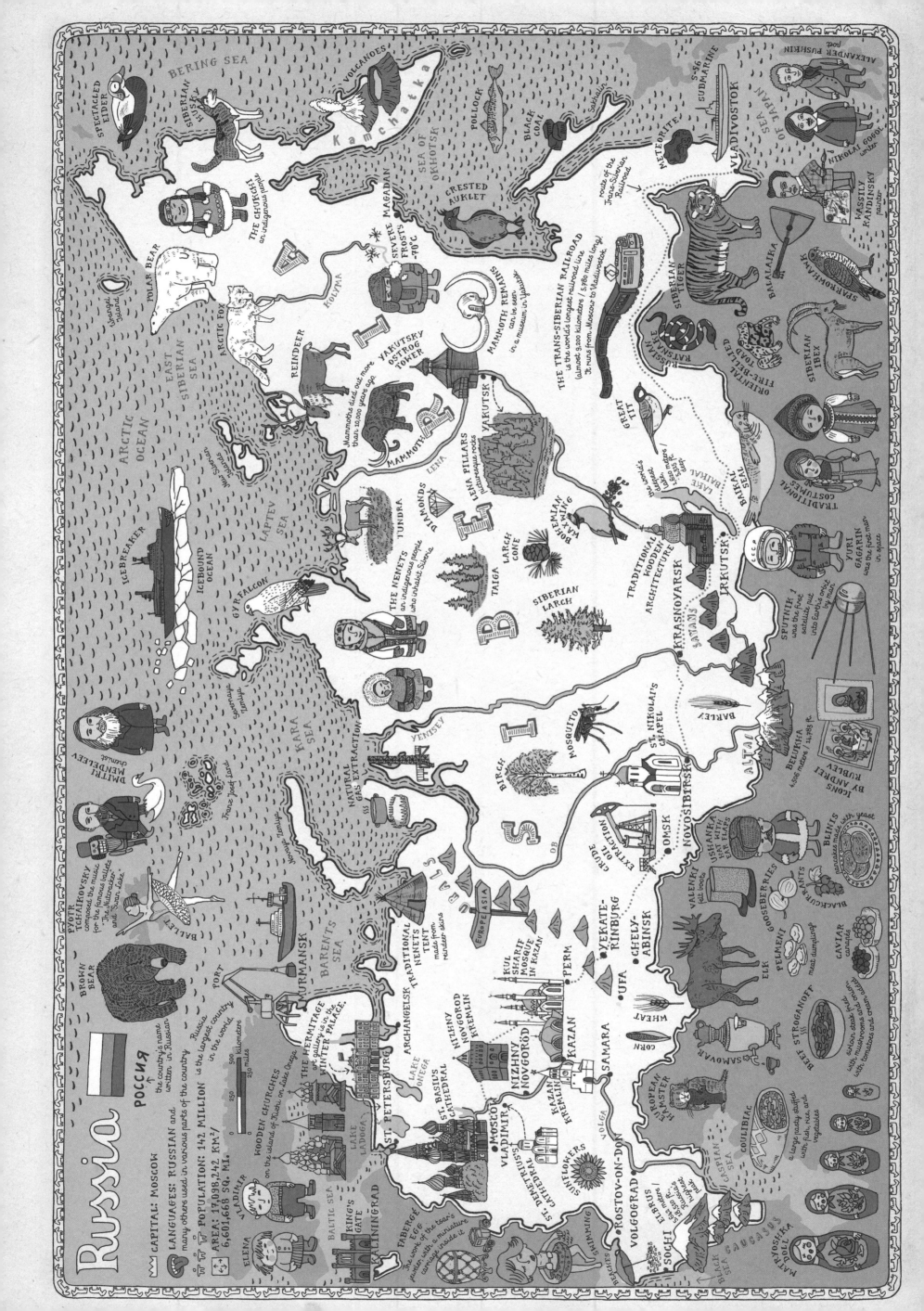

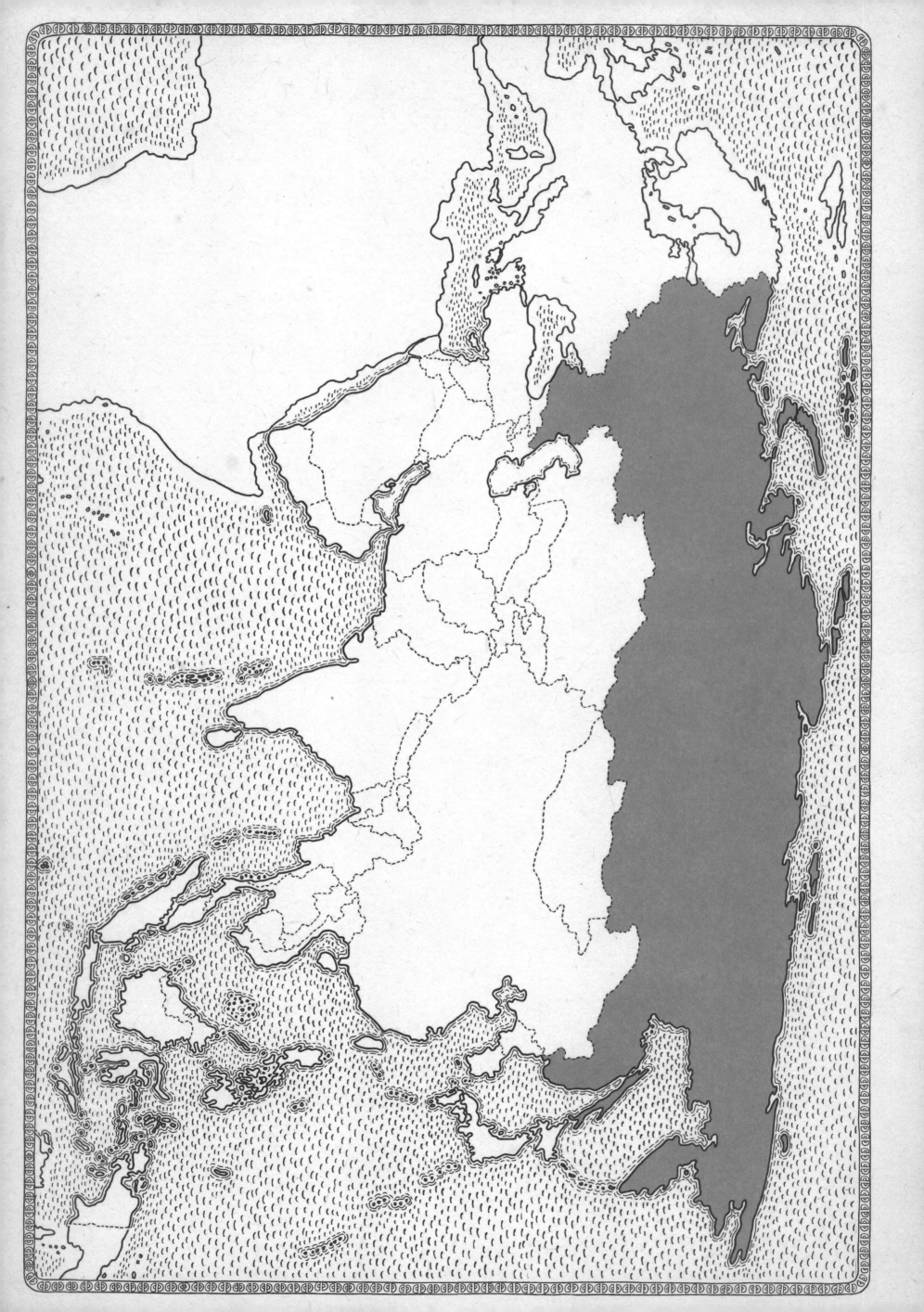

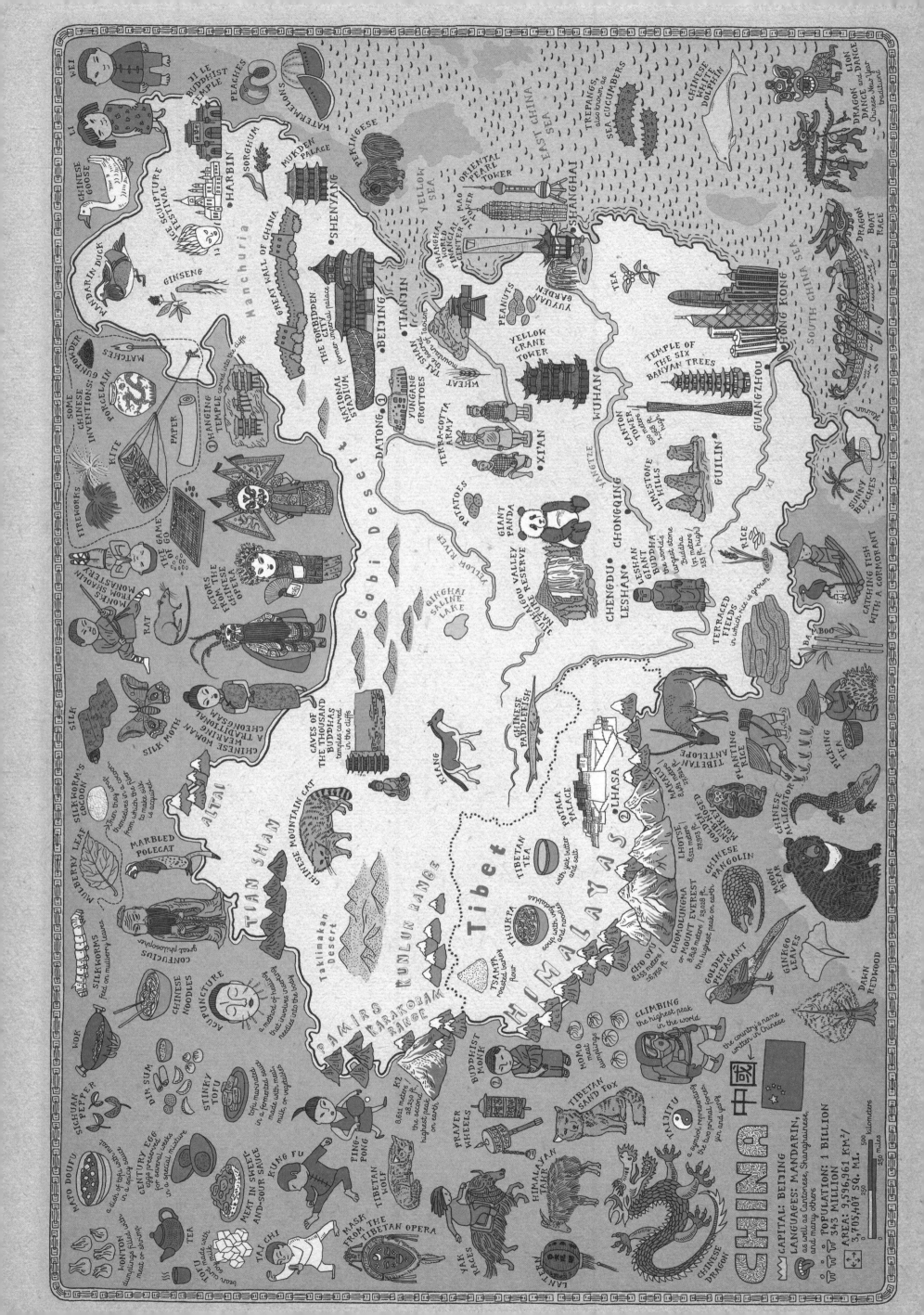

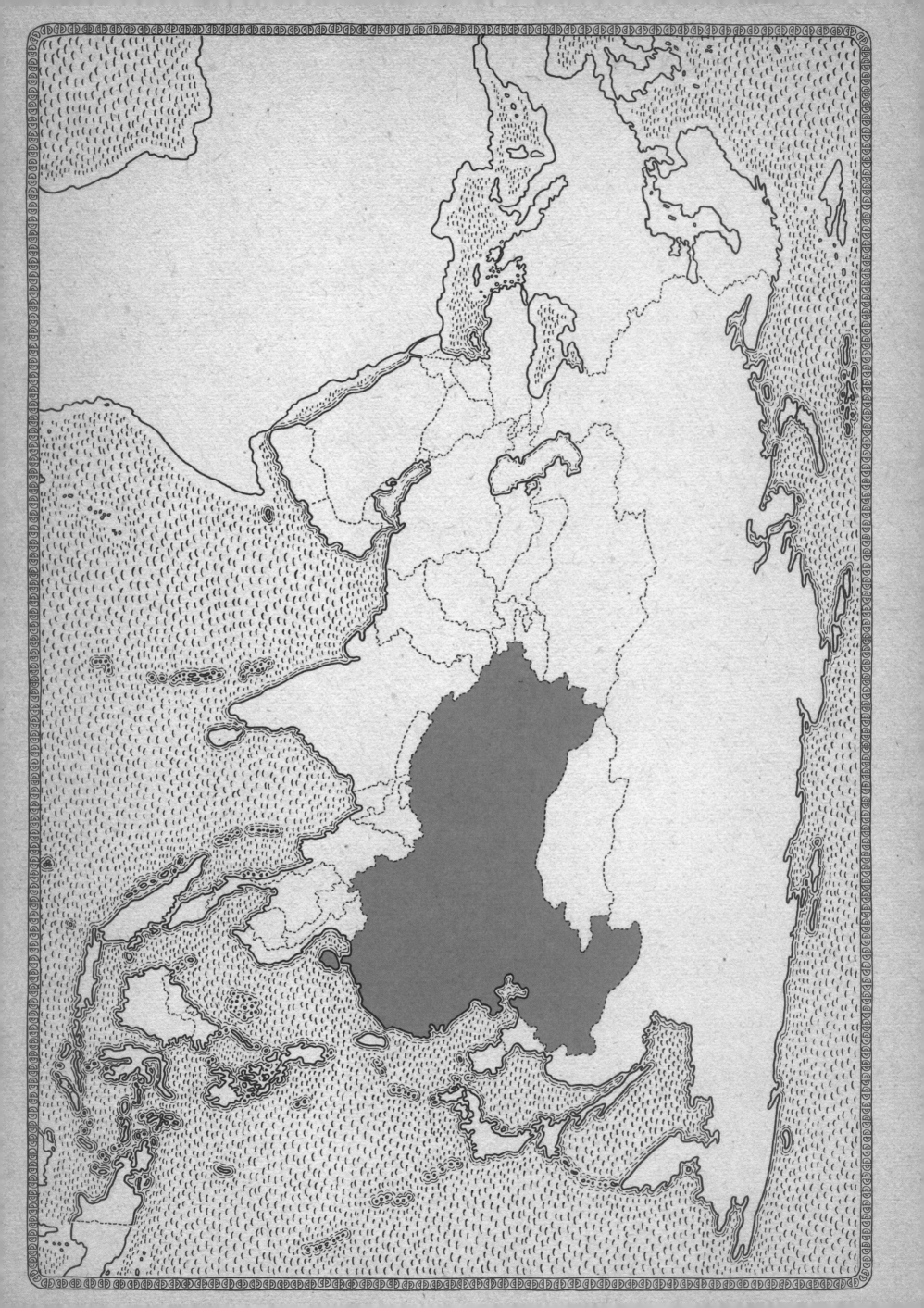

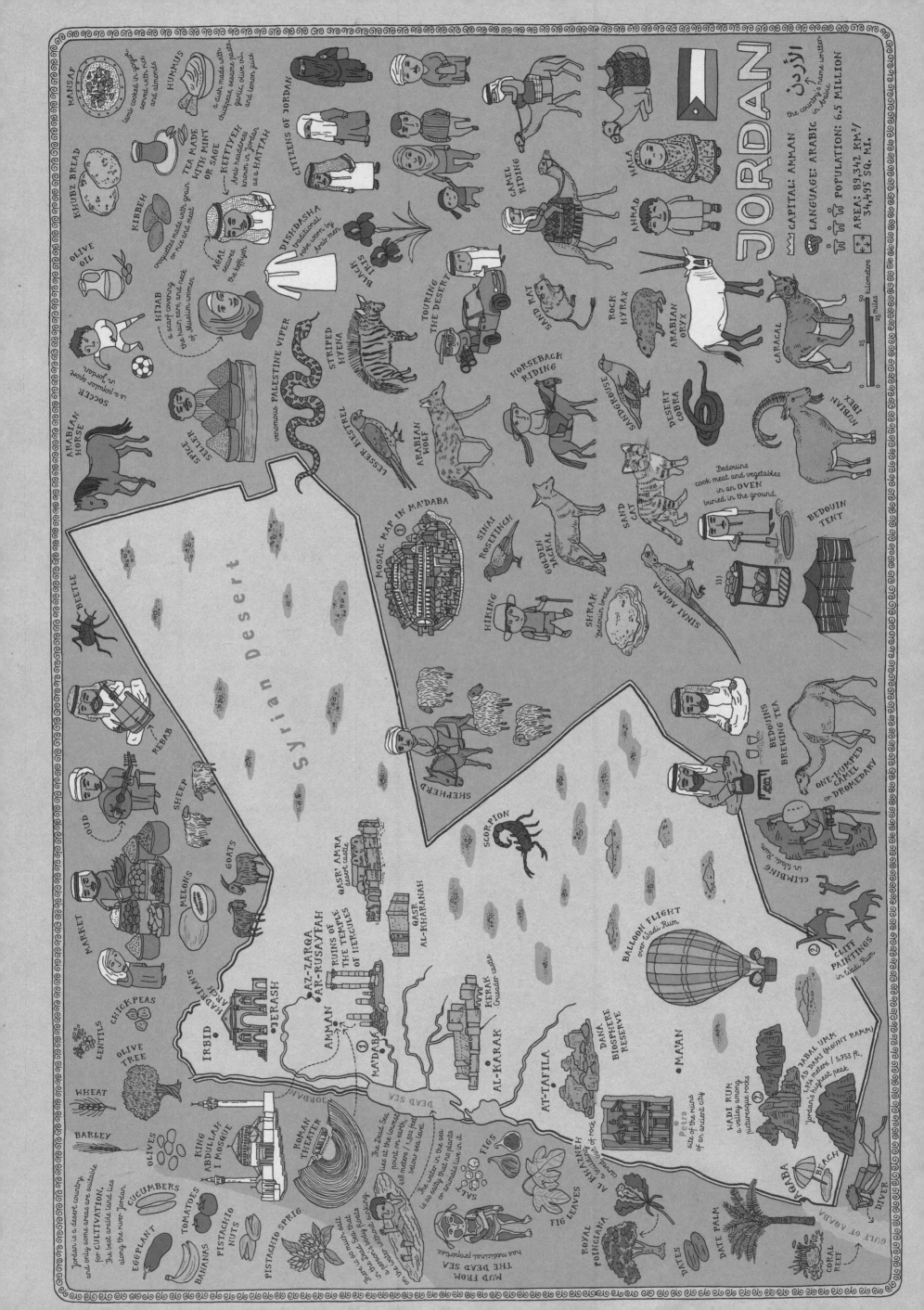

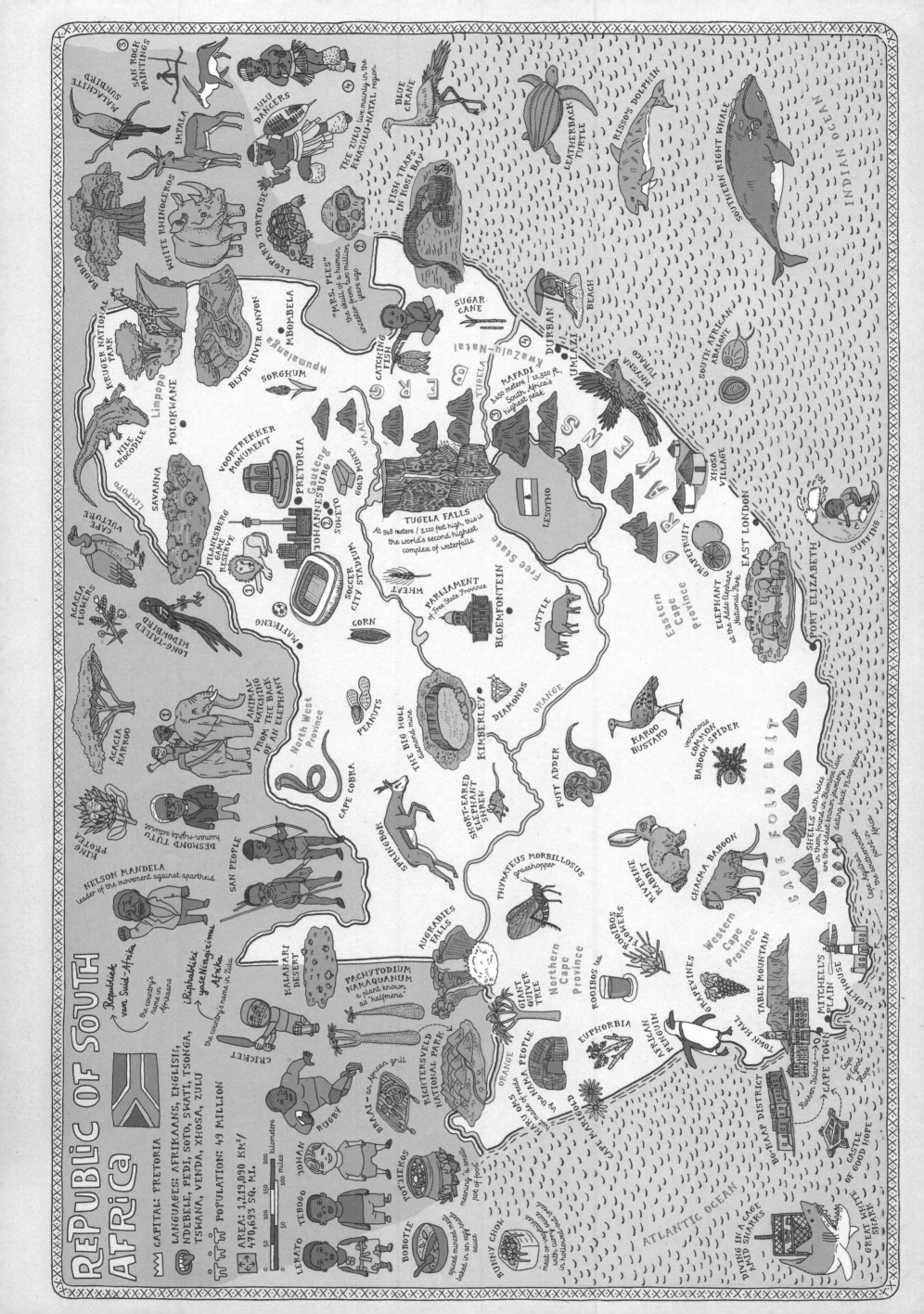

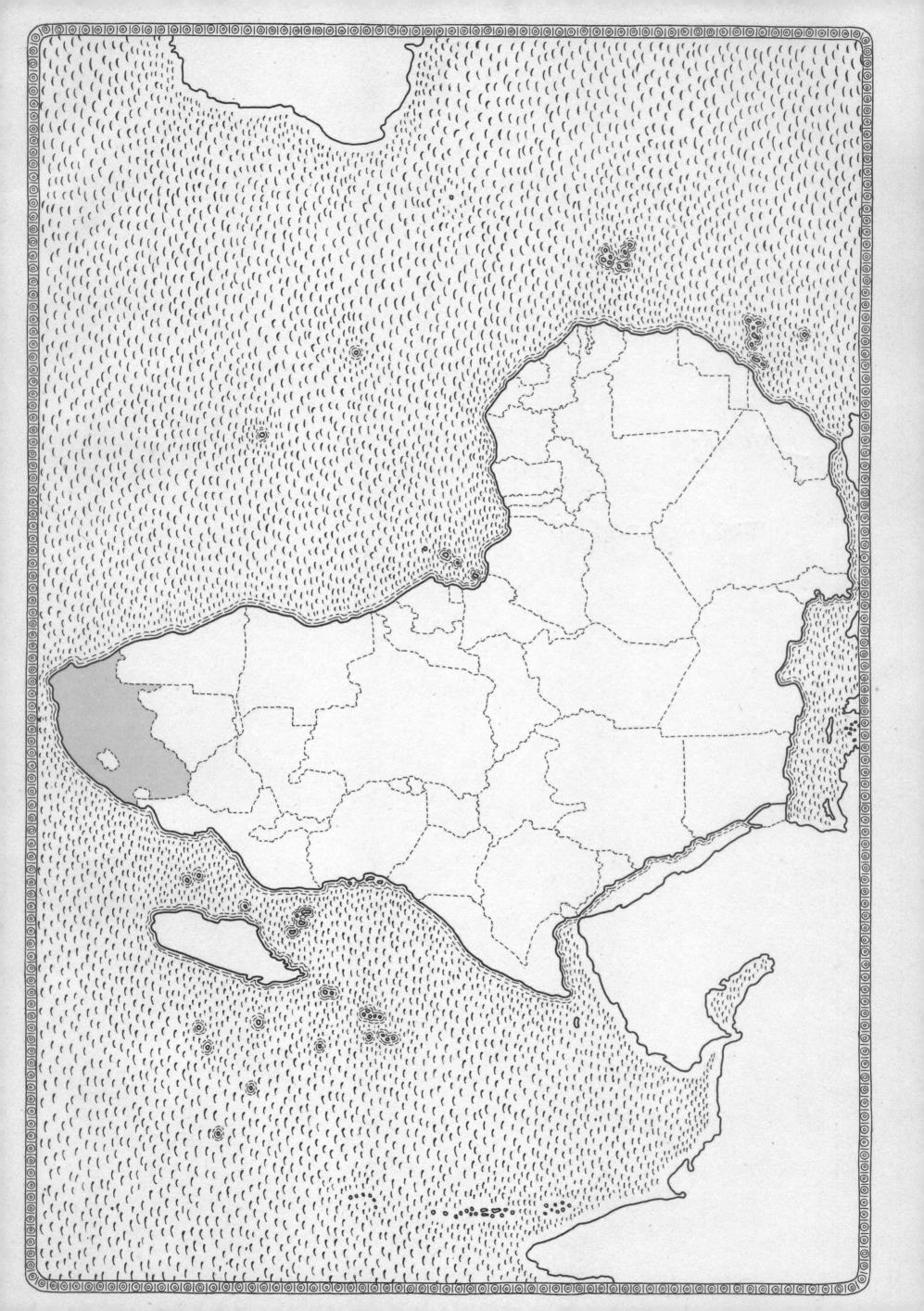

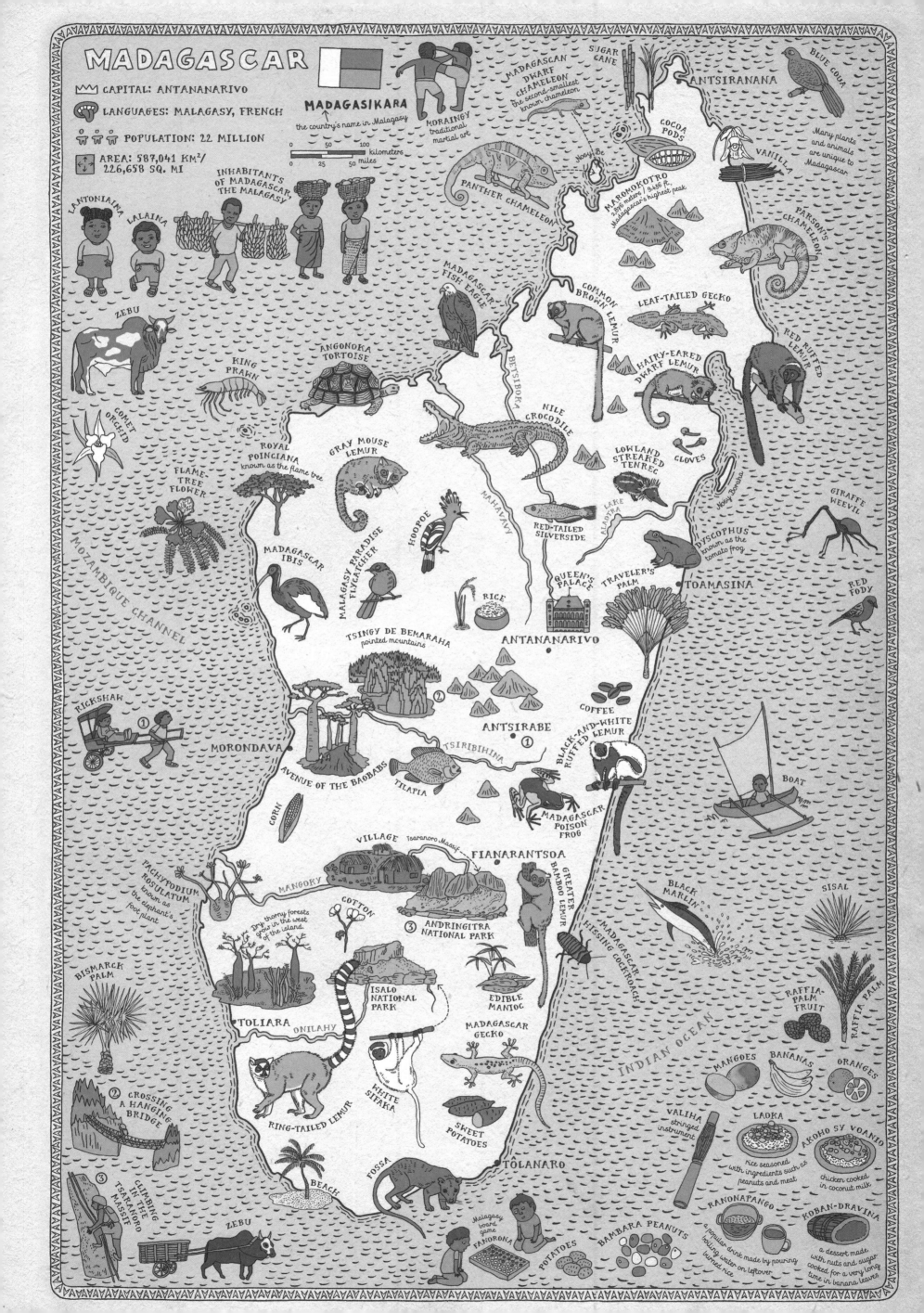

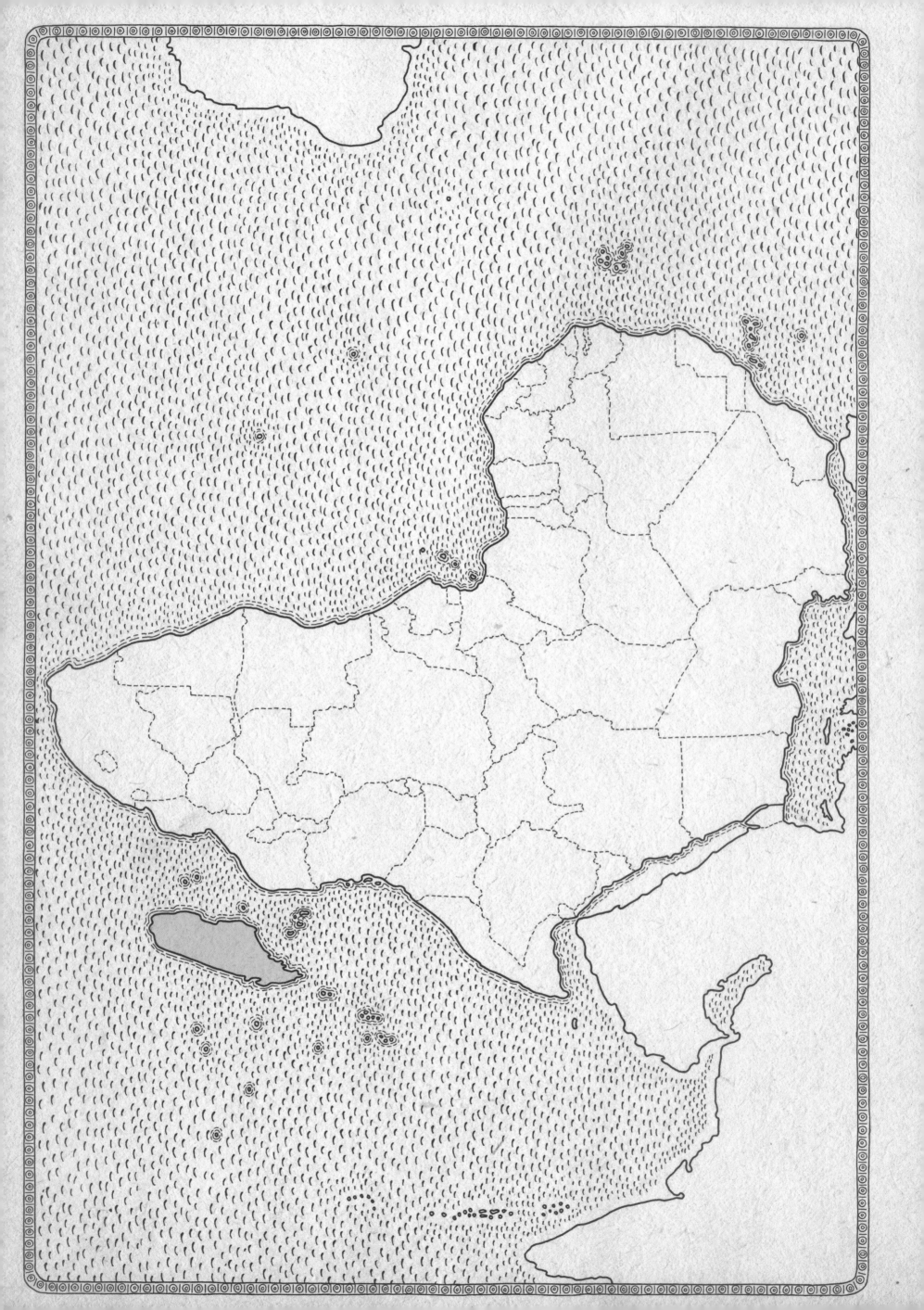

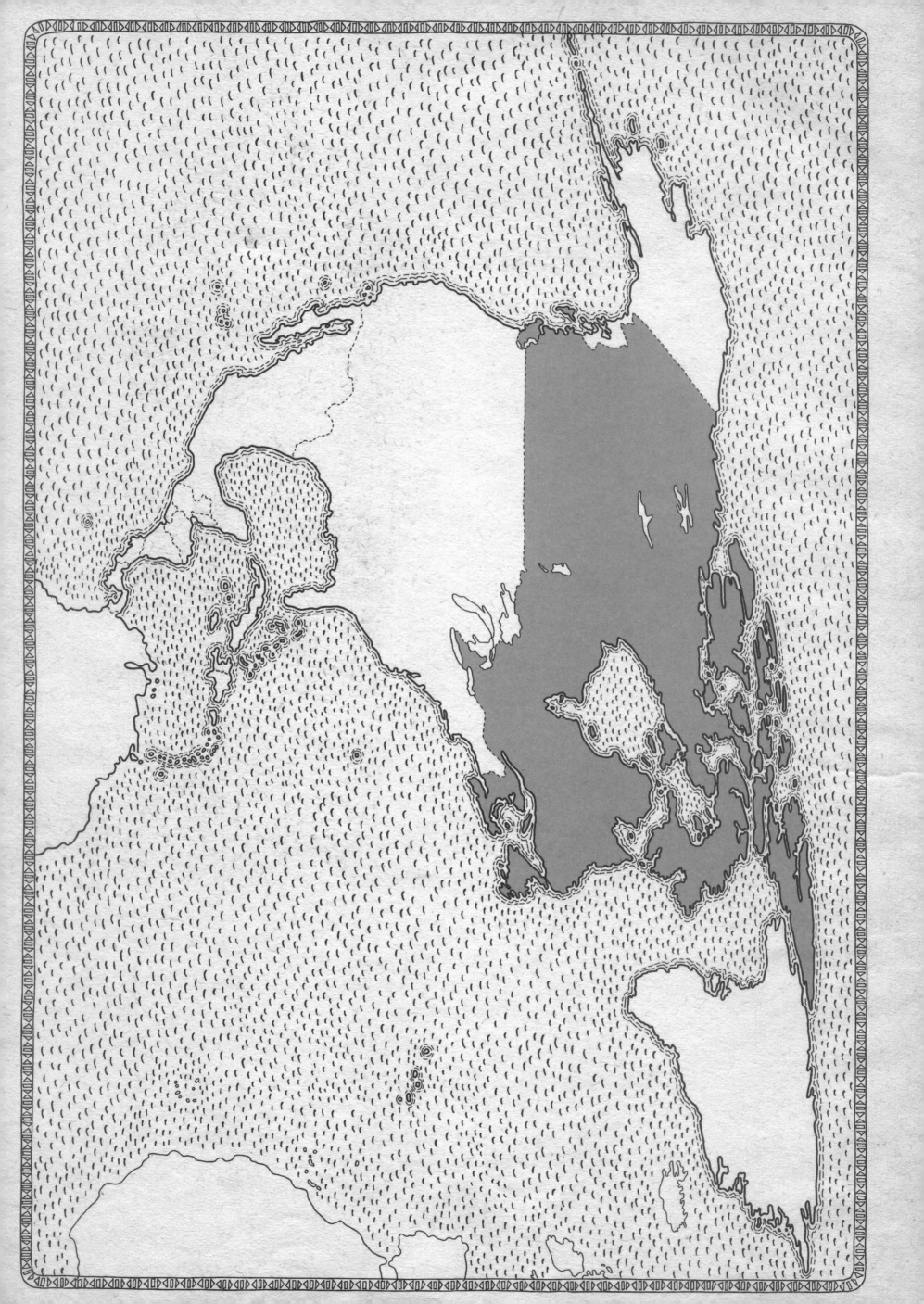

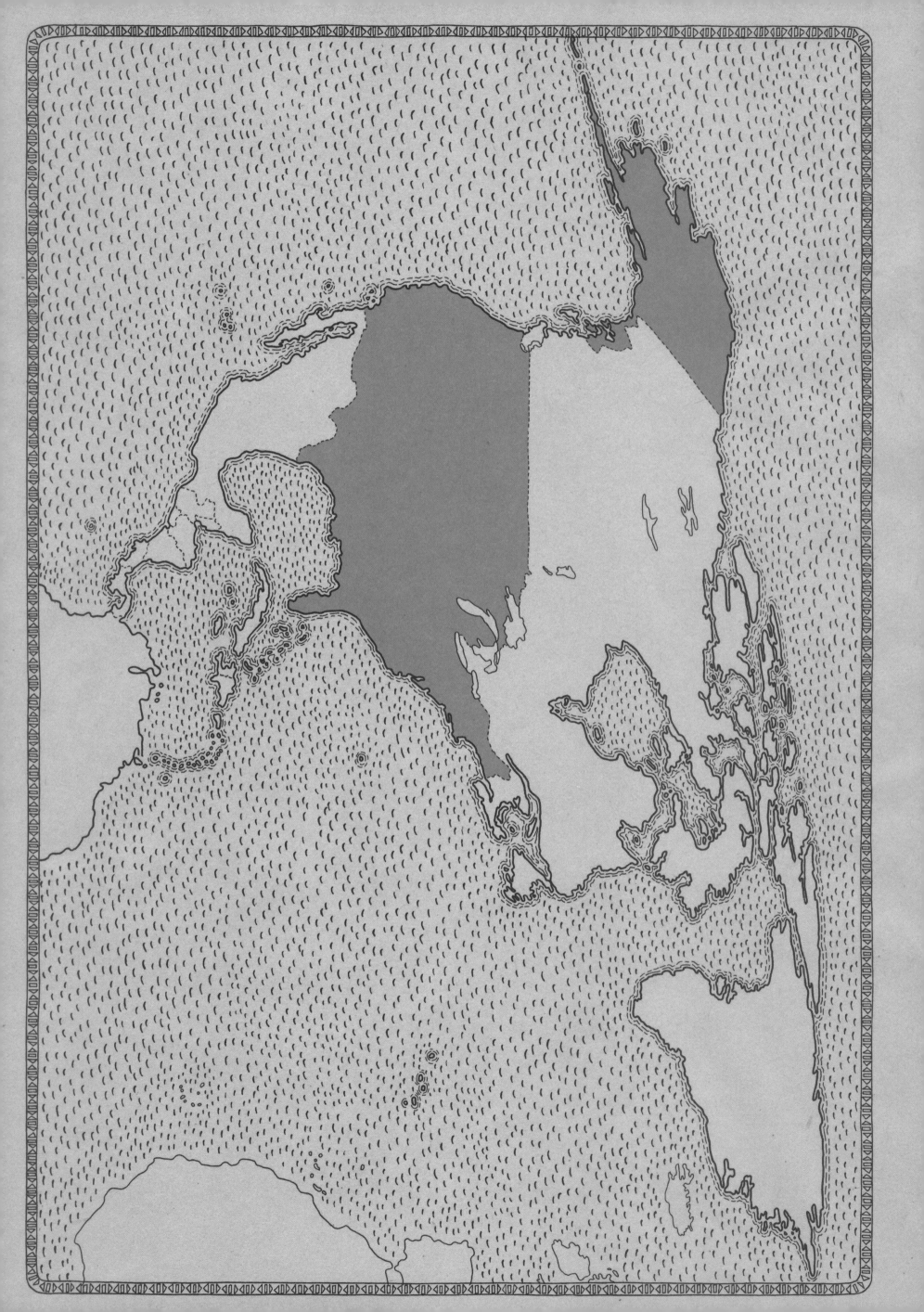

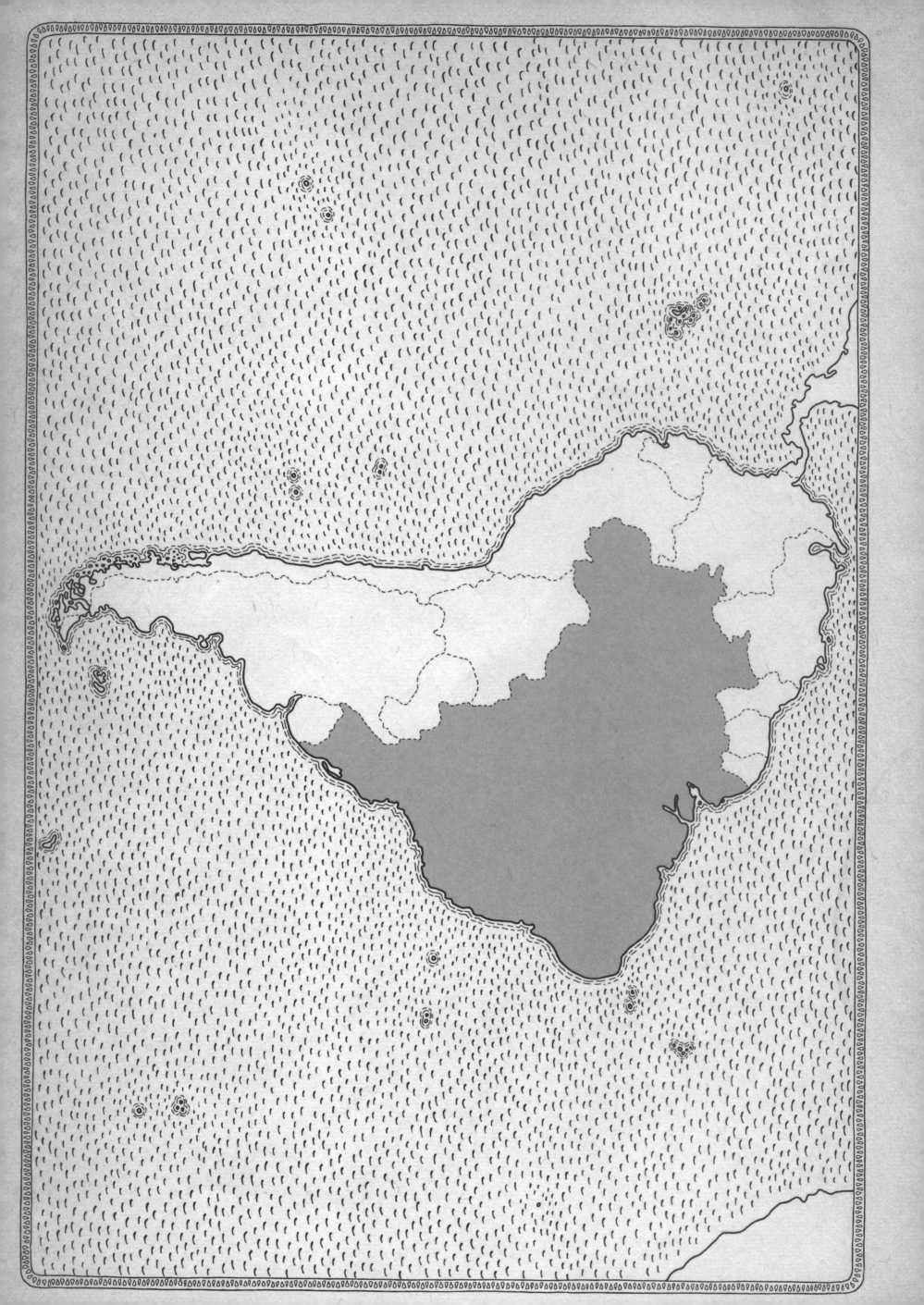

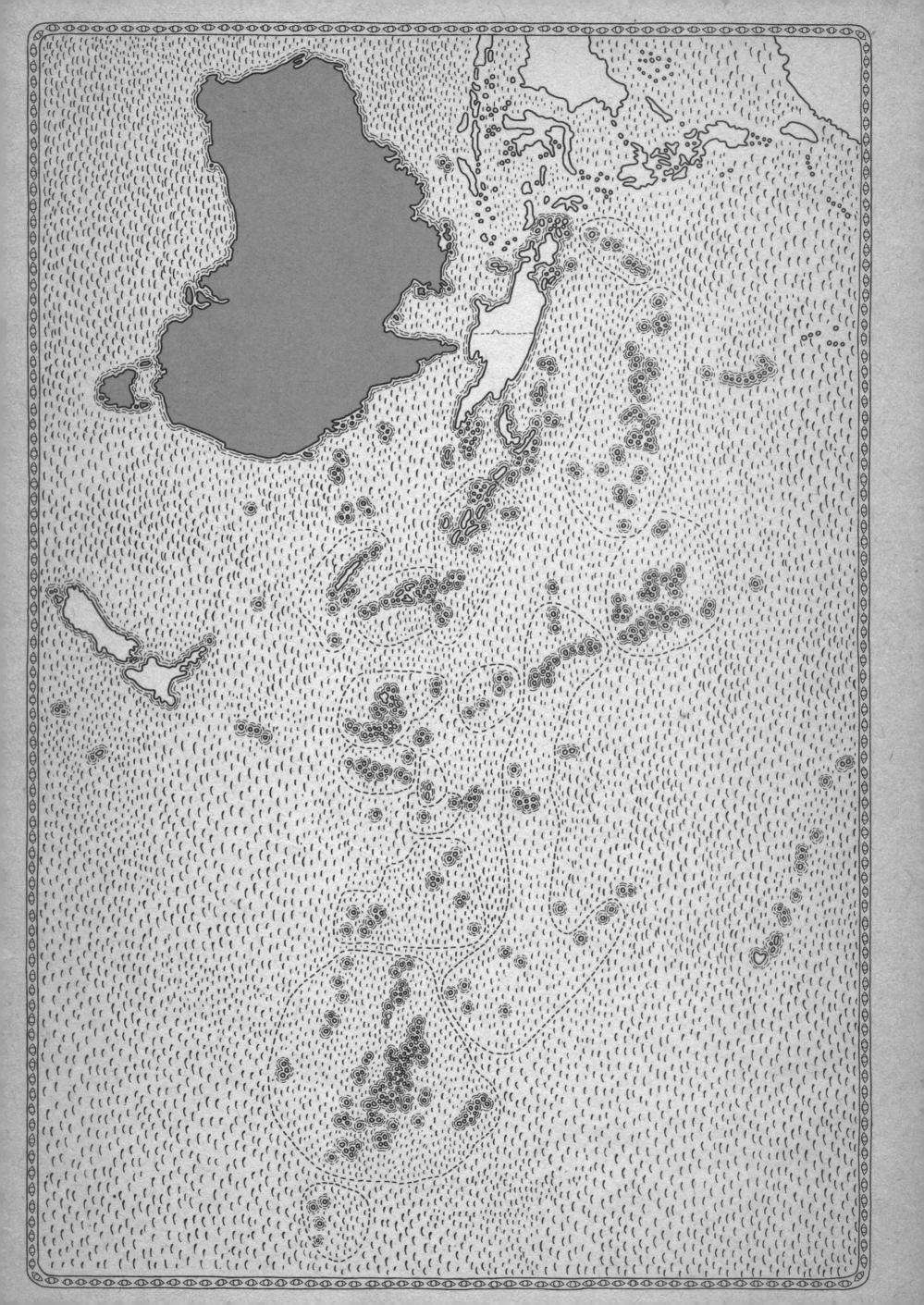

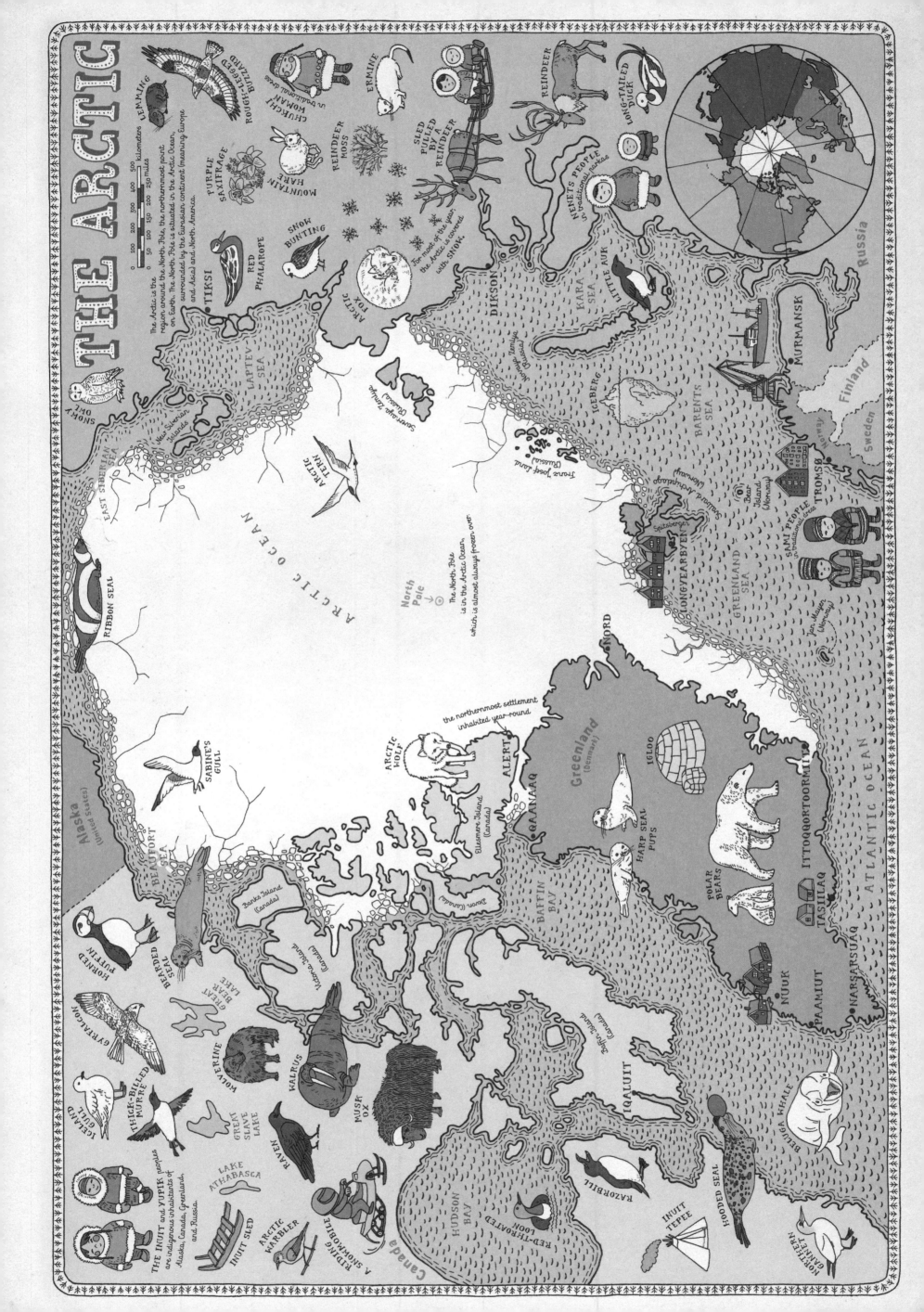

THE ARCTIC

The Arctic is the region around the North Pole, the northernmost point on Earth. The North Pole is situated in the Arctic Ocean, surrounded by the Eurasian continent (meaning Europe and Asia) and North America.

The INUIT and YUPIK peoples are indigenous inhabitants of Alaska, Canada, Greenland, and Russia.

For most of the year, the Arctic is covered with SNOW.

The North Pole is in the Arctic Ocean, which is almost always frozen over.

North Pole

ARCTIC OCEAN

Labels and place names

LEMMING
ROUGH-LEGGED BUZZARD
CHURCHI WOMAN in traditional dress
ERMINE
SLED PULLED BY A REINDEER
REINDEER
LONG-TAILED DUCK
PURPLE SAXIFRAGE
MOUNTAIN HARE
REINDEER MOSS
NENETS PEOPLE in traditional parkas
SNOWY OWL
TIKSI
RED PHALAROPE
SNOW BUNTING
ARCTIC FOX
LITTLE AUK
ICEBERG
KARA SEA
DIKSON
Novaya Zemlya (Russia)
LAPTEV SEA
New Siberian Islands
Severnaya Zemlya (Russia)
ARCTIC TERN
Franz Josef Land (Russia)
BARENTS SEA
MURMANSK
Finland
Russia
Sweden
Norway
TROMSØ
SAMI PEOPLE in traditional dress
Svalbard Archipelago (Norway)
Bear Island (Norway)
Spitsbergen
LONGYEARBYEN
GREENLAND SEA
Jan Mayen (Norway)
EAST SIBERIAN SEA
RIBBON SEAL
SABINE'S GULL
ARCTIC WOLF
the northernmost settlement inhabited year-round
ALERT
NORD
Greenland (Denmark)
IGLOO
QAANAAQ
Ellesmere Island (Canada)
HARP SEAL PUPS
POLAR BEARS
ITTOQQORTOORMIIT
TASIILAQ
ATLANTIC OCEAN
Devon (Canada)
BAFFIN BAY
Alaska (United States)
BEAUFORT SEA
HORNED PUFFIN
BEARDED SEAL
Banks Island (Canada)
Victoria Island (Canada)
GREAT BEAR LAKE
Baffin Island (Canada)
NUUK
PAAMIUT
NARSARSUAQ
IQALUIT
BELUGA WHALE
GYRFALCON
ICELAND GULL
THICK-BILLED MURRE
WOLVERINE
WALRUS
MUSK OX
RAVEN
GREAT SLAVE LAKE
LAKE ATHABASCA
Canada
ARCTIC WARBLER
INUIT SLED
RIDING A SNOWMOBILE
HUDSON BAY
RED-THROATED LOON
RAZORBILL
INUIT TEPEE
HOODED SEAL
NORTHERN GANNET

Scale bar

100 200 300 400 500 kilometers
50 100 150 200 250 miles

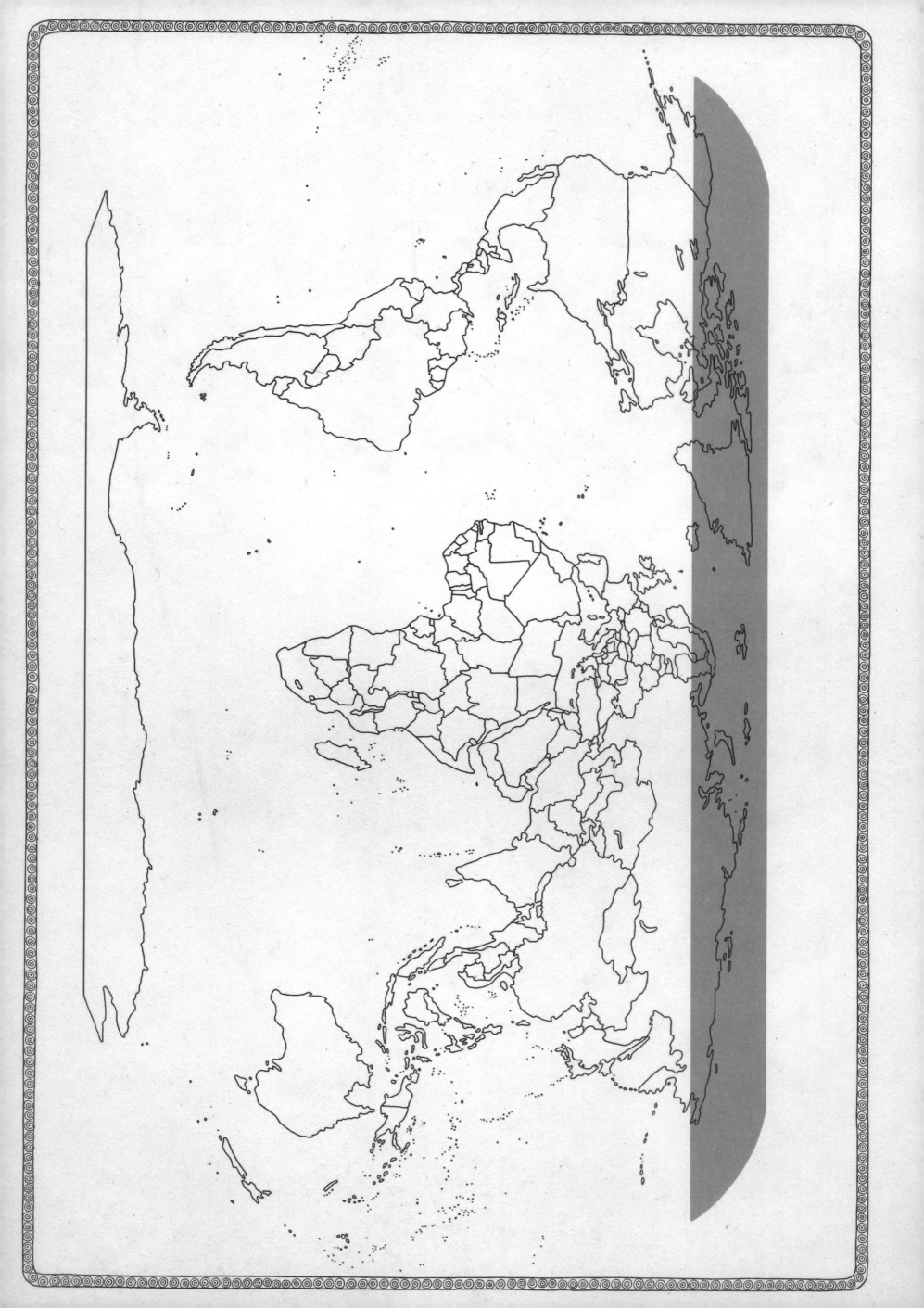

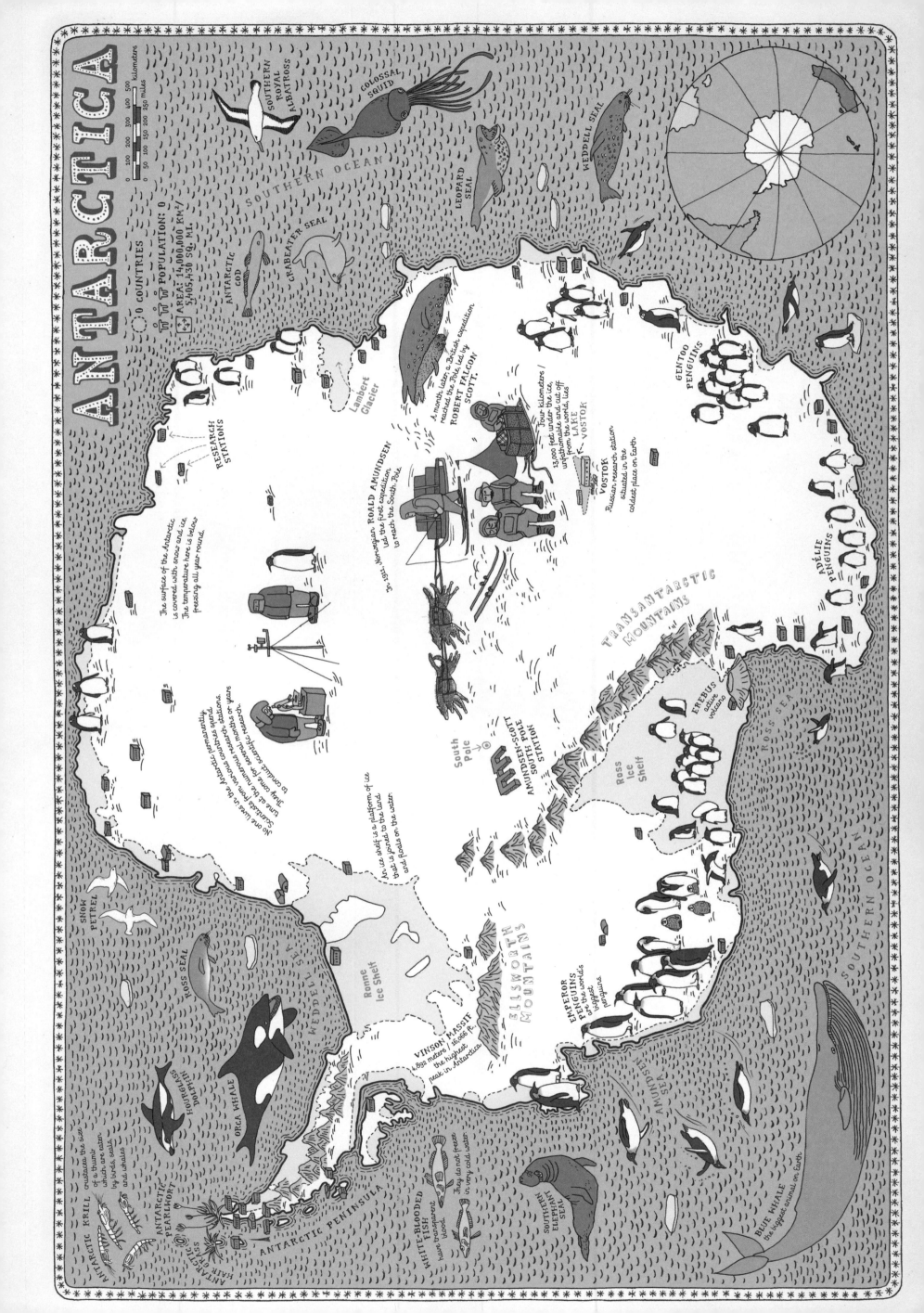

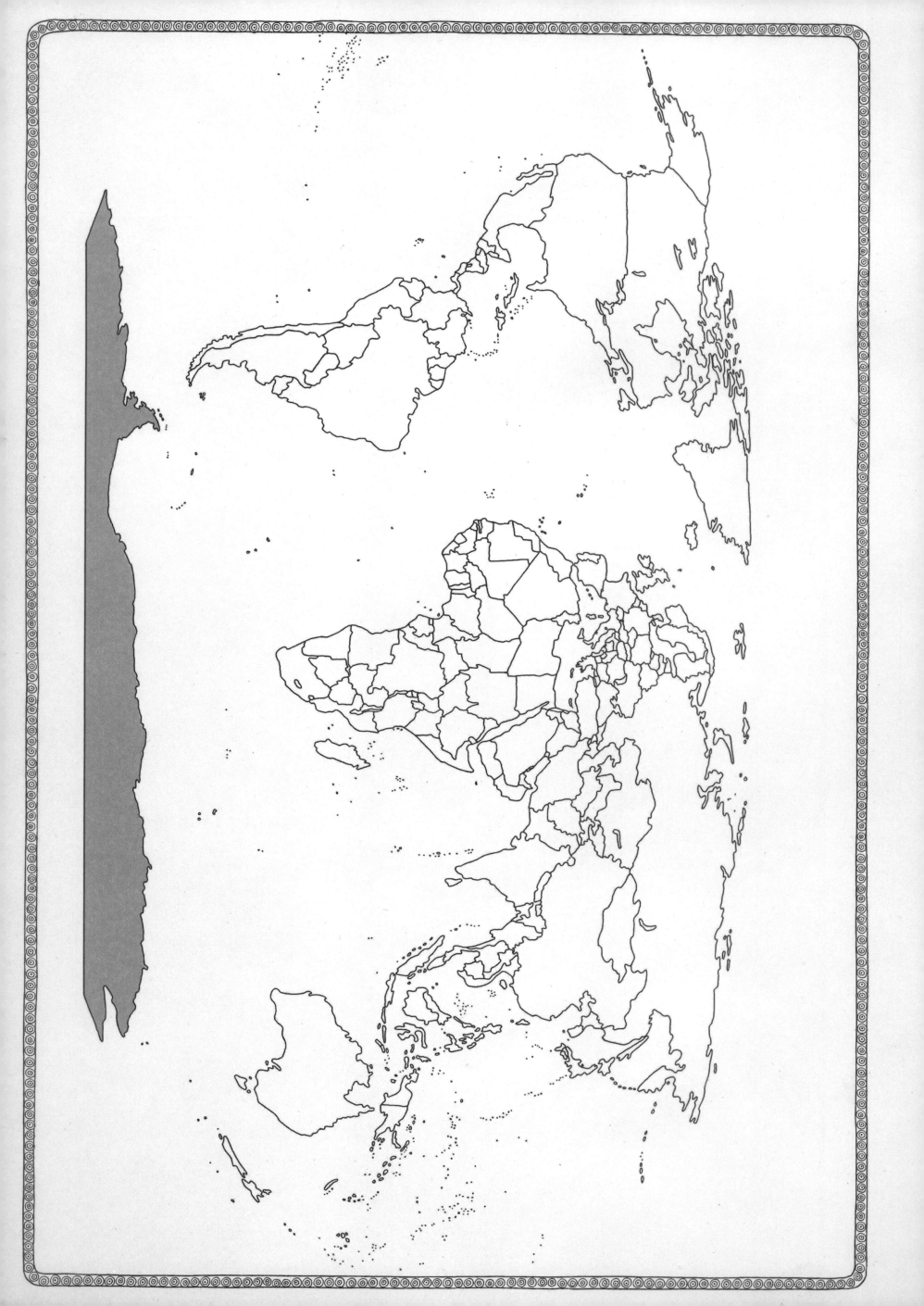